RAISING NATIONS

Parenting Kids with Kingdom Purpose

RHEANNA J. ARFSTEN
2024

For more related articles, tools, and online resources, visit our website at:
www.occupy-freedom.com

Book Interior and E-book Design by Amit Dey (amitdey2528@gmail.com)

ISBN-13: 9798345261422

DEDICATION

This book is dedicated to the only One who knew me before time existed, the One who accepts me for everything I ever was or ever will be; The God of my beginning, my end, and my in between; Jesus Christ. Let every keystroke within this book glorify Your name!

"While we try to teach our children about life, our children teach us what life is all about."

– Angela Schwindt

CONTENTS

Foreword ix

Acknowledgments xi

Preface xiii

PART 1: PARENTING KIDS WITH KINGDOM PURPOSE . . 1

1. Raising Nations .3

2. Becoming an "Ologist" 11

3. Lead the Way 23

4. Don't Give Up, Just Surrender! 35

5. Intentionality 49

6. Cultivating Kingdom Culture 67

7. The Funny Thing is... 83

8. Investing in the Tweens, Teens, and Beyond 93

PART 2: IMPARTING A KINGDOM WORLDVIEW 117

9. Setting the Table 121

10. So Many Questions! 143

11. Father, Son, and Holy Spirit 159

12. Original Design. 177

13. Into all the World. 191

About the Author 199

Endnotes 201

FOREWORD

An urgent text message just came through. Meanwhile I'm being summoned by a two-year-old from the bathroom down the hall needing to be wiped, while my baby is whining, signaling its naptime, and my eldest child is asking the same question for the eighth time. Oh, and someone needs to make lunch and pick up the tornado that swept through the living room before "hangry" takes this scenario to a whole other level.

Welcome to the joy and the privilege of the daily labor of raising nations.

It's interesting how many times in these moments of overwhelm- which happen in a myriad of ways in each season of parenthood- I so easily succumb to it. I've thought, *"I must be the ONLY parent who works this hard, loses their temper, is totally exhausted, and has kids with such stinky attitudes!"* There's nothing like parenthood to pick away the religious crust to expose the bare bones of desperation for the Holy Spirit's intervention. I find myself left with simple prayers like, *"Help me Jesus!"* Even as a Christian mother with a well of Biblical knowledge and a love for the presence of God.

The mundane is where we find ourselves living the majority of daily life. It's why having a kingdom perspective is of the utmost importance to wield these seemingly insignificant moments into something eternal. I've had the privilege of walking alongside Rheanna for almost a decade and through her example and ministry she has been a relational plumb line who anchors my spirit to the kingdom's reality and draws my attention back to the Word in such a way that has brought transformation to my parenting as well as other areas of my life.

Handfuls of times the Lord has used Rheanna's words to cut through confusion and despair to bring the light and refreshment of the Gospel. Almost daily I can see threads of her Biblically-based and inspired council bearing fruit in my heart and home, and I believe this book will leave the same "trail of treasure" for you. Raising Nations goes beyond a good parenting tool, it initiates transformation.

Like me, there are fathers, mothers, grandparents, and spiritual mentors in need of a spiritual defibrillator to "shock" us back to life to become conduits that infuse our homes with the fragrance of heaven and the good fruit of righteousness, peace, and joy in the Holy Spirit. (**Romans 14:17-20**)

I sense we're being ushered into an era, whether it's shepherding needy newborns, wayward teenagers, or our adult children, that parents will step into grace to be constantly aware of Heaven's reality. The grace to abide in the vine (**John 15**) while raising our children will unlock strategies that captivate them with God's love and cast vision for a life of adventure with God.

Rheanna and Justin live out these principles and the generations after them are a testament to that. I'm filled with expectation for you as you turn to the pages ahead that you will encounter new grace, day by day, to raise the precious nations in your care.

Be Blessed!
Brooke Peterson
Well Women Collaborative

ACKNOWLEDGMENTS

I want to thank my husband, Justin, my best friend, the one who has known me at my worst, but only sees the best in me through the eyes of God. We've done great exploits with the Lord together and raising our nations has been among the greatest! You've been in my corner, loving me, and cheering me on every step of the way, I absolutely adore you, mi amore.

To my four nations: Maiya, Evelyn, Matthew, and David, you have always been my heart, my inspiration, my drive, my purpose, and my training grounds. Thank you for extending grace in my failures and teaching me what it means to love, forgive, and receive the kingdom like a child. I am so thankful that God saw fit to let me be your mama and walk this journey with you.

Thank you to the many friends that surround me, pray for me, fight for me, encourage me, believe the best in me, and cheer me on through thick and thin. I could not be the woman I am today without your grace, love, and support.

PREFACE

Though the workings of these pages have been a beautiful burden on my heart for over three years, I believe now is a specific time and season when we are seeing increased evidence of the natural nations, even America, raging against God as mentioned in **Psalm 2:1**. Yet, as the nations of the world rage against God, there is a Kairos season for the Body of Christ, who is the spiritual nation; the holy kingdom of priests that Peter mentions in the second chapter of his first letter. Being possessed by God, we are a nation called out of the darkness and into the light to proclaim the praises of Jesus. I sense that God, in His great mercy, is circling back and highlighting the importance of these holy nations, as well as the transfer of the kingdom to the next generation of nations: our children.

This book is not written with the intent of giving you all the right answers to becoming a perfect parent nor parenting perfect children. I am in no way an expert and I assume no high status on the matter. As a parent, I fail, I fall, and I am still learning. I say things I regret, I make mistakes, and I lay them at the feet of Jesus. I am simply a mother of four amazing nations; children who have been teaching me the art of humility and grace for over twenty-five years. As is promised in James chapter one, I cried out for wisdom, and God answered me and taught me by His Spirit how to be a steward of these nations that He has entrusted to my care. This book is an acceptance to God's invitation to give away what He has freely given to me. So rather than looking at these chapters as a golden ticket to the pinnacle of parenting success, I ask you to receive it as a humble offering of the wisdom that I've learned and am learning along the way.

Always remember that God could have chosen anyone to be the steward of your children, and He chose YOU! Wherever and however you began your journey of parenthood and family, God has a unique plan of redemption for you and your children through a passionate pursuit of Christ together. God has destined your kids for this time and season, and He has given you the privilege of walking with them as they discover who they are and Who they belong to. I pray that something within these pages would make an eternal deposit in your spirit, helping you walk through the doors of intimacy with your children and learning to lean on your Father in Heaven for all that you need. He's got this!

PART 1

Parenting Kids
with Kingdom Purpose

CHAPTER 1

RAISING NATIONS

*"If you want to change the world of tomorrow,
invest in your children today."*

I didn't expect to love being a mom as much as I do. My mom and dad divorced when I was just a baby, and as a child I always felt I was in the way; my process seemed like a burden to the lives of my parents. I know my mom loved me, but she confided on occasion that she didn't think she should have had kids, it just felt like the next thing she was supposed to do in life. My parents did the best they could with what they had, and I honor them for that. Even so, I remember them struggling to enjoy the process of parenting; they were overwhelmed, agitated, and stressed out much of the time. With the wounded perception I carried upon entering motherhood, I assumed parenting would be mostly rigorous, frustrating, and depleted of joy or fulfillment; I perceived it would be mostly duty and very little satisfaction, yet I had a longing for a big family. It wasn't until I met Jesus and started healing from my own hurt and pain that my eyes would be open to the incredibly adventurous and fulfilling mission of raising nations. The last 25 years of walking with my children have been so full of purpose, joy, restoration, connection, and fruitfulness, that I do wonder how my life would have ever been as richly blessed without them. God gave me a mindset shift, opening my eyes and my heart to behold the potential impact that the next generation possesses, and it came in an unexpected way... over lunchtime.

One of the things I have loved the most about being home and homeschooling our four kids over the years is our daily lunchtime conversations. When they were little, we would huddle around our small black kitchen table each day, and in between bites of peanut butter-honey sandwiches and veggie straws they would share their joy with me through giggles, voice their opinions on spiders, ask about heaven and hell, or dissect and question the lyrics to a particular song playing in the background. As each one of them grew, our lunchtime conversations took on different forms, but no matter the question asked, they were open books; they would start chatting and then visit every rabbit trail, open every door to their heart, and share the inner workings of their mind for hours. I would listen to them as they shared and often think to myself, *"there is so much impact this child is going to have beyond themselves, and they don't even realize it yet."* It was in those lunchtime conversations that the Holy Spirit would teach me how to see beyond the toddler, the young child, the teenager, or the young adult in front of me, and catch a glimpse of the nation they belonged to.

THE INDIVIDUAL AND THE WHOLE

You're going to hear the word *nation* quite consistently throughout this book, and you might be wondering what I mean by it. The Holy Spirit inspiration behind the title of this book comes from **Genesis 25:23** when the Lord speaks to Rebekah about the twin boys she was carrying, "TWO NATIONS ARE IN THY WOMB..." A nation, by definition is,

> "A LARGE BODY OF PEOPLE, ASSOCIATED WITH A PARTICULAR TERRITORY, THAT IS SUFFICIENTLY CONSCIOUS OF ITS UNITY TO SEEK OR TO POSSESS A GOVERNMENT PECULIARLY ITS OWN."[1]

Whoa. Let's read that again: a large body of people associated with a particular territory…that is sufficiently conscious of its unity…to seek or possess a government…peculiarly its own. Raising Nations is, in some sense, a play on the words *individual* and *whole*; it means that when we raise our children, we must consider the individual while simultaneously seeing beyond the individual to the whole that God is calling them to.

As we search the scriptures, we find these same words that jumped out from the definition of a nation reaching to us from the word of God, leading us to discover our destiny as a holy nation in Christ. We understand that God calls us each a member of one *Body* (**Romans 12:5**) and a *peculiar people* who are set apart (**1 Peter 2:9**), because we uniquely contribute to the function of the whole kingdom. God will not bless disunity; therefore, He urges us to *consciously preserve the unity* that finds its origins in His Spirit (**Ephesians 4:1**), meaning we must allow our belief in Christ and the power of the Holy Spirit to strengthen our bond as a people, rather than finding unity in our fleeting personal preferences. We are exhorted a multitude of ways in scripture to *seek* the Lord (**Jeremiah 29:13**) because the *possession of our true government* is found in Him (**Isaiah 9:6**) and He rewards those who diligently seek Him (**Hebrews 11:6**).

"Raising nations means that when we raise our children, we must consider the individual while simultaneously seeing beyond the individual to the whole that God is calling them to."

Because a nation is formed by a large body of people who share common mission or identity, it's important to be intentional about the nation you choose to become loyal to and raise your family to become centered around. Nations and nationalism can take on various forms; nations can be based on physical location, political government, ethnic groups, economic systems, social systems and more. As Christians, if we want to understand our heritage as believers and the kingdom nation that we are called to defend, take ground for, and uphold, then we must search the scriptures.

> "BUT YOU ARE A CHOSEN PEOPLE, A ROYAL PRIESTHOOD, A <u>HOLY NATION</u>, A PEOPLE FOR GOD'S OWN POSSESSION, SO THAT YOU MAY PROCLAIM THE EXCELLENCIES OF HIM WHO HAS CALLED YOU OUT OF DARKNESS INTO HIS MARVELOUS LIGHT." - **1 PETER 2:9**

Holy Nation: The unity that we share as believers is that we are called to holiness; to be consecrated and set apart for God; to love and be loved by Him, and this universal calling builds us into a holy nation. We are raising our children to become a part of this holy nation in Christ. The kingdom we defend is holiness; we are possessed by God and not man. I will expound on the topic of kingdom worldview more in part 2 of this book.

> "BUT OUR <u>CITIZENSHIP</u> IS IN HEAVEN, FROM WHICH ALSO WE EAGERLY WAIT FOR A SAVIOR; THE LORD JESUS CHRIST."
> – **PHILIPPIANS 3:20**

Citizenship: A citizen is defined as a "native member of a state or nation who owes allegiance to its government and is entitled to its protection.²" Positionally we are citizens of heaven; seated with

Christ in heavenly places (**Ephesians 2:6**) and geographically we are citizens here in the earth. Both citizenships hold significance, and both are instructed in the scriptures. Being a citizen of heaven means we are born of eternity, we belong to eternity, and our goal is eternity, we are simply sojourners on earth as the Apostle Paul put it; foreigners just passing through. Because we are a people of God's own possession, our positional citizenship is always primary to our geographic location, therefore, our mission is always focused with eternity in mind; this is the "why" behind kingdom-impact parenting. It's important to understand that as a holy nation, we are commissioned to tackle issues with a kingdom government, under kingdom protection, using kingdom principles, so if we want our children to live beyond worldly circumstances, we must teach them to govern the earth from a kingdom perspective. We must raise our nations to understand that their position in Christ is primary to cultural demand. When we help them understand the truth of their heavenly citizenship, they will better understand how to be *in* the world and not *of* it.

> "THEREFORE, <u>WE ARE AMBASSADORS</u> FOR CHRIST, AS THOUGH GOD WERE MAKING AN APPEAL THROUGH US; WE BEG YOU ON BEHALF OF CHRIST, BE RECONCILED TO GOD." – **2 CORINTHIANS 5:20**

Ambassadors: An ambassador is defined as a "diplomatic official of the highest rank sent by a government to represent it on a temporary mission, as for negotiating a treaty[3]." You are seated in heavenly places. You've been given the highest rank in the earth and the authority in Christ. God is making an appeal through you and your children; you are negotiating salvation to the world, YES and AMEN!!

ETERNITY IS THE GOAL

We understand that we are a holy nation; ambassadors of God with heavenly citizenship…and we are going to die someday. Our culture considers it morbid to talk about death because it's considered to be a curse, but we know that Jesus conquered death so it's no longer a curse but a transition from life to LIFE for us who believe. This transition is the most important part of our story as resurrection people! One of the greatest shifts we can have in how we impact our nations in this lifetime for all eternity is to embrace the reality that our assignment here on earth is temporary. Often, we allow stress, anxiety, and depression to overtake us because we get hyper-focused on the temporal issues of this life. We want to impress our social circles with how well parented and impeccably raised our children are, yet our assignment is not to impress but to impact. When we spend too much time trying to impress others, we miss the opportunity to create eternal impact. But, if we keep our eyes set upon eternity in Christ and remember that ultimately, we have been given a short time here to make a big impact, it sets us free from fussing about small things that only serve to distract our true mission. Be careful not to spend too much time teaching your children how to live well and fail to teach them how to die well. This is the reality that you are imparting to your nations; eternity is the goal.

FORCES OF NATURE

Someone or something will shape your children, let it be YOU! It's important for us to understand that the assignment is not simply parenting our kids to become functional adults or positive contributors to society, the underlying truth is that these children are in fact kingdom nations, destined by God, born into this earth for such a time as this. They are inheriting this current culture with the purpose of leading people to Jesus and colonizing the kingdom of heaven here on earth. God has given us an invitation as their stewards to partner with Him and ground them in their calling to love Him and be loved by Him, to train them in their purpose, and to release them into their kingdom assignments. If we do not do this, there is an entire worldly culture full of influence who will do it for us and guaranteed we will grieve the results.

"If we don't shape our kids, they will be shaped by outside forces that don't care what shape our kids are in." – **Dr. Louise Hart**

Raising Nations is not just about individual parenting tactics, better behavior techniques, or the best way to raise a healthy, functional child. Whether you have biological, adopted, fostered, or spiritual children or grandchildren, this book is meant to challenge you to have a kingdom lens when you approach the assignment of parenting and accept the invitation to steward their heart. it's more about raising our children to understand the greater plan they are a part of; the Body of believers they belong to, the nation they are in communion with. When we raise nations instead of individuals, we are teaching our children how to impact, unify, and invest in the greater plan and purpose of God, which is to share the gospel that He might possess a nation of people of His own calling.

PRAYER:

Father, I worship you as the Creator of the children that you have entrusted to me. I recognize these little humans are more than flesh and blood; they are nations of Christ being brought up to know Your love and bring it to a lost and dying world. I acknowledge and accept that the assignment you have given me is not to simply parent their physical but to steward their soul and lead them by the Spirit. I say YES to Your invitation, and I partner with You in this mission. I receive Your great grace to give me all that I need to walk in wisdom every step of the way and I trust you with their today and tomorrow. I give You all glory in Jesus' name, AMEN!

REFLECTION/DISCUSSION QUESTIONS:

1. What is the difference between parenting a child and raising a nation for God?

2. How does this affect your approach to relationship with your children?

3. What are the things in my life I need to shift to be more eternally minded as I raise these nations?

CHAPTER 2

BECOMING AN "OLOGIST"

Ologist; suffix: "an expert in a particular area of scientific study."

I t had become a family tradition over the years, that on Sundays after morning church we would invite friends to go out to a restaurant and share a meal, enjoying rich conversation and great food together. We would talk about life, faith, family, and God dreams. On one particular Sunday we sat at the Green Mill eating a sausage pizza, discussing our kids, who at the time were ages 10 and under. We chatted about the ins and outs of who they were; their learning styles, personalities, expressions of affection, and some challenges and victories that we had with each one. Mid-conversation our friend paused and looked at me intently and said, *"Wow, you're quite an "ologist" of your children!"*

"An ologist?" I questioned.

"Yes!" He replied, *"you seem to know your kids inside and out and really understand their personalities; how they learn, what they like and don't like, and what makes them tick. When I hear you talk about them it makes me think of an 'ologist'- an expert in a certain field of study. Essentially, you are a Maiya-ologist, an Evelyn-ologist, a Matthew-ologist, and a David-ologist."*

I stopped for a moment to ponder what a profound way to look at parenting this was; that instead of molding them into who we think they should be, we can become an expert in their uniqueness; discovering who they are, connecting with them, and guiding them in a customized way. A sacrifice of time, intention, and energy, yes, but what a gift it is for us to take the opportunity to really get to know all the beautiful ways that God has wired them to learn and to grow; learning what they like and don't like, how to love them and receive love from them. God looked through billions of people around the world and saw fit to give your nations to you, because you are the mom/dad that your nations need. It wasn't a mistake. It wasn't chance. He chose you because He knew your strengths and weaknesses were exactly the right fit for their journey. Oh, how beautiful it is when we realize the intentional gift God has given us with our children; it's a treasure to take the time and energy to truly become an "ologist" of each one of them!

> *"The most precious jewels you'll ever have around your neck are the arms of your children."* – **Cardinal Mermillod**

GOD IS AN OLOGIST

When we see the suffix "-ologist" it indicates a person who studies or has expert knowledge of a particular kind of science. Some examples would be a biologist, psychologist, zoologist, radiologist, and many more. When we become an "ologist" of our children it means we devote personal resources to study and know each one of their personalities, their love languages, their expressions, their needs, and their destinies. This is precisely how God studies and knows each one of His kids in such an intimate way, the scriptures say:

- He knows us. (**Jeremiah 1:5**)
- He searches our heart. (**Romans 8:27**)

- He's numbered the hairs on our head. (**Matthew 10:30**)
- He knows our needs before we even voice them. (**Matthew 6:8**)
- He designed every part of who we are. (**Psalm 139:13**)
- We are the apple of His eye. (**Psalm 17:8**)

GROW WITH THEM

Getting to know who your nations are, how they process information, and how they express themselves is essential in understanding their hearts and helping guide them through the tumultuous journey of life. From birth your kids give you cues to let you know there is a need to be filled—or perhaps a need to be changed because their pants are filled. Once they begin to cry and fuss you tap into your inner sleuth and start the process of tracking down the issues; do they need to be fed? Rocked? Changed? Bounced? Burped? You try every possible combination until the code is cracked and the crying ceases. You then give yourself a pat on the back and a gold star in the category of "Baby Whisperer." In these moments you realize that you have officially embarked on the journey of becoming an "ologist" of your nation.

When you have these little ones in the house chances are you are tired. I don't mean a little kitten yawn here or there tired, I mean baggy-eyed, lots-of-coffee, underwear-on-backwards, questioning-the-meaning-of-it-all, tired. Each day you may wake up to conquer the world—and the laundry monster—while each evening you fall into bed, asleep and drooling before your head hits the pillow. The in-between consists of the ultimate quest to take care of every need that presents itself; runny noses, dirty diapers, cuddles, mealtime, play time, snack time, reading time, bath time, dinnertime, and hammer time. The physical demands and the overwhelming number of repetitive little jobs are exhausting. Then as these little nations grow into middle-schoolers, tweens, and teens, the journey of parenting begins to transition from task-focused to relationship-focused. Where you once had control over that little body, you now have opportunities to influence their heart, mind, and direction.

"A parent holds their children's hand for a while,
but their hearts forever."

Whether it's the tasking or the relationship aspect of parenting, you may find yourself stronger in one area over the other. Perhaps like me you're more of an organized detail-oriented person and you thrive in completing small jobs, working off of lists, and managing several different needs at one time. When my nations were little, I thrived in the area of managing daily tasks and schedules. Even though I indeed felt exhausted and needed breaks from the demands, I really felt like I understood that season of parenting. On the contrary as my children got older, I struggled with switching over to a relationship-focused mindset simply because relationships take much more intentional time, personal sacrifice, and mental energy. I had to allow God to teach me how to lean into each season and stage of their growth by stretching and growing for myself; sometimes it was growing in selflessness, learning patience, or letting go of control. It isn't always an easy task, but I have come to realize that if we want to go with them, one way or another, we've got to grow with them.

THE IMPORTANCE OF KNOWING

The world can be simple and affirming, yet it can also be loud and intrusive; the highs and lows of life impact us from all sides. Even when we raise our nations in protective environments, we cannot control all of the circumstances that will shape the narrative of their mindsets. Since kids are just like sponges, they tend to absorb an incredible amount of the stress and information—both good and bad—clawing at them on a daily basis. Depending upon their personality, they'll either openly process that stress with you or tuck it away until intentionally excavated. Because a young person's brain isn't fully developed until they're in their mid-twenties, they tend to struggle with making rational decisions and managing intense emotions. If they do not have someone to draw out their issues and guide them through, over time they can become susceptible to breaking down or blowing up, which can ultimately impact their adult relationships with themself and others.

I grew up in a broken home; my parents split when I was just a toddler and for most of my life they were not on peaceful terms. I was marked by the stress of divorce, strife, addiction, abuse, and instability and often felt the pangs of rejection, displacement, and abandonment. My mom was our primary caregiver and a single parent doing her best to work three jobs, caring for my brother and I, but there wasn't much margin for processing the complex emotions that came along with such a stressful and adverse environment. Because of this dynamic, I didn't fully develop healthy coping skills or learn how to appropriately articulate my feelings. I would grow to become a dysfunctional middle schooler and a rebellious teenager; I lied, cheated, stole, manipulated, and misused others. I was in an incredible amount of pain and felt trapped in the bondage of my emotions due to the fact that I could not effectively communicate or cope, so I acted out often. I was kicked out of kindergarten at five years old and sent to a Catholic school which only compounded the rejection I felt. In middle school I was often invited to youth group and then kicked out for being disruptive. Finally in high school, after multiple run-ins with the law and school authorities it was decided that I would be placed on ADD medication because they didn't know what else to do. At the age of 22 I gave my life to Jesus and started the journey of healing my soul. I began to unpack the pain of my wounds, build a healthy emotional IQ, and learn how to appropriately communicate my thoughts and feelings. Most of my healing took place through the simple act of conversation with someone who was willing to take the time to listen, affirm, and guide my process. My testimony of growing up has served as a sobering reminder to me of the importance of knowing my kids. Our God-given relational role in our nations' lives is an important one that can make the difference in their process, giving them the grace to understand and be understood.

> *"A fool does not delight in understanding, but only in revealing his own mind."* **Proverbs 18:2**

Because the world can be noisy, confusing, and provoking, it's significant to take the time to listen to your nation's feelings and thoughts no matter how ridiculous they sound to you at the time. Doing so—without interjecting your opinions—could bring them the peace they need to process through their emotions correctly. Giving a patient and listening ear is also how we help our nations build emotional intelligence, which gives them the confidence they need to communicate their feelings, likewise becoming comfortable with the feelings of others. It's important to know your children and act when you see warning signs of pain and repressed turmoil. Don't stop pursuing them even when it feels futile; pray and ask good questions until their issues are drawn out and dealt with in a healthy way.

THE ART OF COMMUNICATION

We live in a high-tech culture with every kind of advanced contact possible, however somewhere along the way it seems we have lost the art of meaningful communication. We can somehow say everything without really saying anything, we can hear everything without really listening to anything. Through social media, television, internet, and smart phones, we live in a constant state of noise, but simultaneously we can be some of the most isolated and disconnected people on the planet. The unattended consequences of this state of living are depression, loneliness, anxiety, and addiction. Putting away electronics and having meaningful conversations with your nations is a foundational element of a deep relationship with them. A meaningful conversation means heartfelt focus on the person you are with, it's getting past the surface to the deep things, it's listening before you speak, understanding before you're understood, and it requires healthy margins in your life. Opportunities for meaningful conversations with your nations may often come at very inconvenient times, but they hold the potential of priceless growth and influence. Meaningful conversations can be hard conversations, so you must be willing to yield yourself to uncomfortable topics and questions such as sexuality, questioning faith, stewarding possessions, drugs and alcohol, and personal struggles. I often lean into the "Law of first mention" when it comes to hard topics like these. This principle is often used when studying the scriptures and it embraces the idea that if you want to understand the context of a particular word, imagery, or story, you must go back to where it was first mentioned in the Bible. As it pertains to your kids, you want to be the first mention; the first person to teach them the truth of life, love, kingdom, and cultural content, because this will set a proper reference point for them to come back to when they are faced with challenges in those areas. Being willing to communicate with your kids on these types of subjects is imperative in supporting appropriate mindsets; being the first to discuss any challenging topic gives your kids the reference point of truth instead of trend. If we don't spend intentional time communicating with our nations about life, somebody or something else will, and whoever gets there first may just end up crafting the lens of their worldview. Create space in your schedule to have meaningful conversations with each one of your children, you'll be amazed at the opportunities that are presented through letting them share what's on their mind.

INVITE THEM

As a stay-at-home mama my littles were always in tow. Whether it was weekly grocery shopping, doctor appointments, prayer walks, coffee dates, or theatre shows, we did life together. As my kids began growing older, I started enjoying the freedom to get out of the house and run errands by myself, and I could get done double in half the time! However, I began to realize that by continuing to invite them to come with me even though they didn't need to, I had the opportunity to get to know them one on one. It occurred to me that the connection we had that was once convenient would now take more intentionality to maintain. I decided to invite just one kid each week on a rotating schedule, they would be my helper and in return I would let them make decisions on the flavor of yogurt, brand of crackers, and the kind of cereal to throw in the cart, then I would bring them out for lunch at a restaurant of their choice—which was almost always Culvers. Over a cheeseburger, fries, and the flavor-of-the-day, each one of my kids would reveal what was on their heart and mind; sometimes it was the latest trend in NBA player stats, other times it might be sharing the excitement of counting down the days until summer camp. There were deep questions like, *"what does the law of sowing and reaping mean?"* and connection questions like, *"mom, what's your favorite movie of all time?"* Wherever the conversations take us, I value those moments immensely knowing I will never regret getting half of my tasks done in double the time so that I could get to know each of these precious nations that God has given to me.

Inviting your kids into your activities also gives you a chance to model a healthy example of kingdom function; you have the platform to show them generosity in tipping a server, praying for someone in need, or doing what's right in a challenging situation. I remember a scary moment in the grocery store one day when an elderly lady who was standing behind us in line became unconscious and hit the floor. As people rushed to call 911, I crouched over her and began to pray and speak against death. After a couple of minutes, her eyes opened and she sat up, dazed. I returned to my cart with my nations wide-eyed and interested and I was thankful they were asking questions and learning how to run to Jesus in important situations. Whether it's a spa day, car show, bible study, shopping, baseball game, or slaying the spirit of death over someone at the grocery store, take opportunities to bring your kids into your world even when it's inconvenient.

DRIVING 15 IN A 30

One of the greatest keys I've learned in becoming an "ologist" of my nations is to slow down. Like driving 15mph in a 30mph zone taking in the surrounding scenery and feeling every bump in the road, slow down and purposefully absorb the intricate details of your kids' lives. Study their mannerisms; what makes them laugh? Frustrated? Sad? excited? How do they connect with God? Maybe it's listening to music, walking in nature, or reading books. Maiya and Evelyn have found connection to God in music and friendships, Matthew connects through stories, and our younger son, David, loves to connect outside, particularly in the evening. He frequently comes to me, even in the cold winter months and asks, *"Mom, do you want to go on an evening stroll with me?"* He will comment on the feeling of the cool breeze, stop to smell the lilac bushes on the walking path, and gaze into the sky with awe and wonder exclaiming, *"WOW! Isn't that sunset beautiful?!"* Usually he then grips my hand and adds, *"But not as beautiful as you are, mom."* There are times when he comes to gather me for a walk and I'm right in the middle of completing a seemingly important task, it takes everything in me to set it aside so that I can connect with him. I have to remind myself that this young boy is only visiting my life, and someday will be replaced by a strong, self-sufficient man with a family of his own. As I step over how I may feel in the moment of interruption in order to do what I know is good, I never regret the precious quality time I spend with him or any of my four children. Life is full of hustle, high demands, and fast pace, but I encourage you to slow down, look your child in the eyes, gaze at her smile, hear his laughter, hold her hand, and embrace their heart. I assure you; you will never regret driving 15 in a 30 and becoming an ologist of your precious nations.

PRAYER

Father, thank you that You know me inside and out. Thank You that you know my children inside and out as well. Help me to slow down with each moment and tune into who You've created them to be and what You're doing in their lives today and for eternity. I surrender my need for perfection so that I can receive Your grace to be present in their laughs, their cries, their victories, and their challenges. Help me excavate the uniqueness that my child holds so that I can encourage them to grow in it and share it with the world! In Jesus' name, AMEN!

REFLECTION/DISCUSSION QUESTIONS:

1. Ask the Holy Spirit to show you some innerworkings of your children. Write down some ways they handle victory, defeat, thought process etc.

2. What are some unique qualities you notice about each of your children?

3. How can you invite your children into your day-to-day this week?

CHAPTER 3

LEAD THE WAY

"A leader is one who knows the way, shows the way,
*and goes the way" – **John C. Maxwell***

M y journey of motherhood started when I was just 17 years young and a senior in high school. I gave birth to my older daughter, Maiya, via cesarean section in February of 1999, I turned eighteen two months later in April, and then graduated from high school in June with her on my hip. I have a picture of me and her on my graduation day; me donning my purple cap and gown and her in her little overalls, just 4 months old. When she graduated from the very same high school eighteen years later, we decided to re-create the photo with her in her purple cap and gown and me holding her in my arms as a sweet reminder of the goodness of God in our lives.

As a single teen mom working full time and going to part-time college, I met my husband, Justin, when Maiya was around two years old. We dated for a couple of years, fell in love, and got married in August of 2003. Just two months after we got married, we accepted the invitation to place our trust in Jesus, and just seven months after we said yes to Jesus, we had our second daughter, Evelyn. We didn't enter the parenting scene armed with full Sunday school knowledge or years of experience following Jesus, so when it came to teaching our little nations about what it meant to love Jesus, by default we had to lead the way; they learned as we learned. I found out very quickly after I said yes to Jesus and became a mom of four, that I was not the savior of my kids; I was their steward, and after twenty plus years of being a parent I am a firm believer that it's not just about doing/saying the right things, it's about surrendering to the right One. If you want your nations to love Jesus, then let them see you live your life loving Jesus above all else. As my husband says, our spiritual well of knowledge and experience wasn't very deep when we were having babies, so instead of digging it deep *before* we started teaching them, we handed them a shovel, welcomed them into the process and we dug the well deeper together as a family. For us it wasn't a choice, it was what we had to work with, but I have come to realize the necessity of this process for all parents everywhere, no matter how much knowledge and experience you think you have before having kids. It's highly beneficial to raise your nations, not from a high place of knowing it all, but from a surrendered place of growing, learning, and processing. Where you lead, they will follow.

TROUBLESHOOTING

Have you ever purchased a piece of Ikea furniture? If you have, you know what I mean when I say that it's a labor of love to put one of those puppies together. There are usually a gob of screws, brackets, plugs, and wood pegs along with a booklet of instructions that seem to be translated in Greek. One particular occasion, while I was putting together a bookshelf that we had purchased, I began to wonder what it was like for that poor fella in quality assurance who tested the product instructions over and again until he found the right execution. I chuckled to myself, *"oh man, I could never work in that kind of job…"*, and then I realized I do have that job, it's called parenting. Justin and I now have four beautiful nations, our oldest is married with a daughter of her own now. On many occasions, my husband and I have had to apologize to her that she had to be the brunt of much of our big "IKEA" years. As each one of our children walked through the many milestones of childhood, we would make mistakes, and correct them the next time around, so by the time our fourth came, it seemed to my other kids like he was our favorite because there were just less bumps in his road than theirs. We typically respond to these accusations with, *"it's our first-time being parents, and your first-time being kids, there is no blueprint for this process!"* As we have paved the road for our kids to walk, the greatest challenge we've faced is to walk the road for ourselves first, troubleshooting with Jesus, humbling ourselves, and leading by example.

I have always had an easy time *telling* my kids what's right and wrong, but it's the *showing* them by practicing what I preach that I tend to stumble over. Each one of my kids have helped me realize the weaknesses, inconsistencies, and stubbornness of my heart. They have also given me a reason to address the broken places and let God build me into the bridge that will lead the way to Him. There are two important ways that we will lead our nations: words and actions. Words and actions are both very powerful; your words will pave the road and set the road signs, while your action is the car that demonstrates how to drive on the road and obey those road signs. Both word and action must be unified to create impact in your child's life.

"My children, my darling precious children. What I want them to become, I must become myself." – **Elizabeth Prentiss**

THE POWER OF WORDS

> "THE EARTH WAS FORMLESS AND VOID, AND DARKNESS WAS OVER THE SURFACE OF THE DEEP, AND THE SPIRIT OF GOD WAS MOVING OVER THE SURFACE OF THE WATERS. THEN GOD SAID, 'LET THERE BE LIGHT'; AND THERE WAS LIGHT." - **GENESIS 1:2-3**

Words. They're important. They formed the very earth we walk upon, the air we breathe and the life that we live. God spoke, and substance existed, earth was formed, creation emerged, and light dawned. Even you and I are the living, moving and breathing word of God (**Genesis 1:26-27**).

> "SO WILL MY WORD BE WHICH GOES FORTH FROM MY MOUTH; IT WILL NOT RETURN TO ME VOID, WITHOUT ACCOMPLISHING WHAT I DESIRE AND WITHOUT SUCCEEDING IN THE MATTER FOR WHICH I SENT IT." **- ISAIAH 55:11**

God is a purposeful God, and when He speaks, He sends an important assignment with His words. His intentions are to bring life and prosperity, to renew old things, and uproot dead things so that life can spring forth. He promises that every word He speaks will not return to Him without accomplishing what He desires in it, and because your nations are the manifested words of God, there is a destiny on their life; a purpose, a mission, which God declares will not return to Him void. The words you speak to your children and over your children will either support the destiny of God on their lives or attack it. I want to pause a moment and acknowledge anyone who finds yourself in this moment milling over careless or negative words that you have spoken to your children out of frustration or fear. I want you to know that I can relate, this was me; I was the negative, yelling, frustrated mom. Before the training and discipline of the Lord, I used my words as a mother to produce results not fruit. If reasonable boundaries and requests were not getting me results, I resorted to frustrated yelling and threats. I'm not proud of that, and I've had to repent to my children for those moments of failure, but I embrace the weakness of my humanity and believe God restores through repentance. We're all in a growing process, there's grace for it! I still find myself thinking and saying things every once in a while, that are certainly not ideal—if you don't have teenagers yet, you'll know what I mean when you get there—and in those moments, I have to ask my kids to forgive me. Then, I get up and start again. So, if this is you, repent, ask for forgiveness, and get up and start again, God's got you!

> "BUT I TELL YOU THAT EVERY CARELESS WORD THAT PEOPLE SPEAK, THEY SHALL GIVE AN ACCOUNTING FOR IT IN THE DAY OF JUDGMENT." - **MATTHEW 12:36**

Words have the ability to bring life or death, restoration or destruction, faith or fear. Your words are a powerful weapon and tool that God has given you to build, fight, love, conquer, comfort, and encourage the world around you. Because things are set into motion when you speak, you will be forced to respond with action to back up every word that comes from your mouth. In **Matthew 12:33** Jesus admonishes that if the tree is good (heart), the fruit will be good (words/actions), and if the tree is bad, the fruit will be bad. This principle applies to the words we speak over our children, the fruit of what we say will be produced in their heart, whether good or bad. When you find yourself frustrated remember that what you say may very well produce results, but stop to ask if it's producing the fruit you're looking for; are you getting your way or are you making a way for good fruit? Your voice will be one of the loudest voices in your child's head, so use that power wisely!

Statements that Encourage Good Fruit:

- "I'm glad God gave you to me."
- "I believe in you."
- "It's okay to mess up, nobody is perfect."
- "I love it when you help me."
- "You're strong."
- "You're beautiful/handsome just the way you are."
- "You are a great friend."
- "You handled that situation with maturity."
- "You can overcome this!"

Statements that Encourage Bad Fruit:

- "What is the matter with you?"
- "I cannot stand you right now."
- "No wonder they won't play with you."
- "Start acting right."
- "You don't listen."
- "You are so lazy."
- "There's nothing to cry about."
- "You get frustrated over the dumbest things."

THE POWER OF ACTION

Simon Says is a fun and easy game that my family has played out in our backyard on many summer nights. If you're not familiar with the game, it's simple; one person is Simon, and Simon stands in front of the rest of the group and gives a series of quick commands both verbally and visually. Only if Simon says, "Simon says" at the beginning of the command, should the group follow the command, however if Simon does not say, "Simon says" and a person still follows the command, they are out of the game. In addition, if any person does not follow the verbal command correctly, they are out of the game. The last person standing wins. One of the easiest ways I have found to get kids out of the game, is to say one thing while I do another. I'll say *"Simon says hop on one foot"* but instead of hopping, I'll kick my foot and 90% of the time, the kids will follow what they see me doing instead of following what I'm saying, thus getting put out of the game.

"It's not only children who grow. Parents do too. As much as we watch to see what our children will do with their lives, they are watching us to see what we do with ours. I can't tell my children to reach for the sun. All I can do is reach for it myself." − ***Joyce Maynard***

I cannot tell you how many times over my years as a mom, I have heard one of my children say, *"but that's what you do",* or *"that's what dad does",* upon confronting them about a specific behavior or attitude. Yet again it reminds me to take inventory of my own words and behaviors and how they align with the character of Christ. What you say holds power, and what you do carries influence with your nations. They are forever looking out for the fruit of your life to speak continuity with what you're preaching to them, because they want to believe you, they want to follow you, it's a natural instinct for them to hang on to your every step. The challenging piece to this parenting puzzle is that in order to have a positive influence in your child's life, you're going to have to surrender to Jesus; be willing to learn, grow, and be held accountable to your actions. We'd all love to believe that if we just tell our kids the right things to do, that they'll listen regardless of what we do with our own lives, but this couldn't be further from the truth. Just like "Simon Says" their eyes are listening more than their ears. If you tell them not to text and drive, but then you text and drive because you just HAVE to get that message sent, guess what? They'll likely text and drive. If you tell them to stay away from doing drugs and drinking alcohol, and then proceed to talk about all the fun you had as a teenager doing such things, guess what? They may be tempted to try it. Why? Because your kids trust you, and if you find it appropriate enough to add it into your life, then they don't see any issue with it, even if you've told them that it's not right. I'm not saying we must be perfect; in fact, it's good for our children to know that we mess up because it gives them confidence to find grace in the mess-ups as well, but practicing an inconsistent lifestyle of words and actions will cause issues especially as they grow up. As your kids become more aware, your words will lose power and influence simply because they are now mature enough in mind to see that they cannot trust you if your words and actions are inconsistent. You must first be willing to face the changes you need to make in your actions and attitudes before you can have influence to instruct your nations in the same way. If you want to teach them a positive quality, then you must lead the way with influencing actions!

> *"Don't worry that your children never listen to you; worry that they are always watching you"* – **Robert Fulghum**

Influencing Actions:

- Generosity – give more than you take.
- Love – sacrifice more than you require.
- Forgiveness – receive and extend grace for mistakes.
- Humility – say *"I'm sorry"* without adding excuses.
- Strength – protect others publicly and confront them privately.

- Intelligence – share the knowledge you have with others.
- Joy – laugh and have fun!
- Peace – when storms come, stand on the word, practice what you preach.

If you've screwed some things up, here's the good news; your children love you, and God loves you! So, when you mess up, and you will, go humbly and honestly before God and your kids to repent and ask for forgiveness. It's a good thing to admit to your kids when you're wrong, the act of humility teaches them something very valuable; that it's okay to be imperfect, and there is always room for growth!

What you say today will shape their tomorrow,
and what you DO to back up what you say,
will influence them for a lifetime.

LET THEM SEE YOU

How do we lead the way by word and action? The greatest piece of wisdom that I can give from experience is to let your kids see you in process. Do not hide from them; let them know you are human and that you are just as committed to growing and learning as you are encouraging them to be. Your nations will learn most by lifestyle; if you want to teach them to pray, then let them see you pray. If you want to teach them humility, then be quick to apologize to them without excuses. If you want to teach them to be generous, then let them see you give generously. If you want to teach them the importance of studying scripture, let them see you open your bible every day. If you want to teach them compassion, let them see you cry and let them comfort you. If you want to teach them grace, then respond with grace to the guy who cut in front of you at the check-out line. If you want to teach them how to kick the devil in the teeth, then go on and let them see you war, declare victory, and fight spiritual battles. If you want to teach them faith then invite them to believe God with you for something, so they can see His provision and favor. Be vulnerable with your kids, and they will be vulnerable with you. Talk with your kids about your thoughts and feelings—with discretion, and they'll share theirs with you. They will interact and respond to you in the measure in which you interact and respond to them.

There are instructions, guidance, and bits of wisdom I find myself offering to my children, and as I verbalize this guidance, I simultaneously take an inventory of my own actions to be sure that I have the influence to back up the guidance. I understand that If I'm going to talk, I better be willing to walk, otherwise I'm just throwing things out and hoping something will stick. Leading the way will take intentionality, humility, and resolve, and it will bear the good fruit of a good tree.

PRAYER

Jesus, I worship You as the ultimate Leader! You know the way; you are the Way, and you went the way. You are the first fruits among the dead and you've paved the way to life and eternity. Instill in me a heart to lead well; to not just demand performance from my children, but to be humble enough to go first. Examine my heart, Lord, and find any way within it that needs healing, deliverance, and restoration so that I might show my children the way of following in Your footsteps. Help me be an arrow to Your throne in all that I say and do. I receive great grace in my weakness to walk in Your power every step of the way. In Jesus' name, AMEN!

REFLECTION/DISCUSSION QUESTIONS:

1. Your children learn about Jesus first by the example of your lifestyle and personal pursuit of the Lord. So, how are things between you and Jesus?

2. How are you speaking life into your children? What fruit is being produced?

3. Where do your actions need to be strengthened with passion for Jesus?

CHAPTER 4

DON'T GIVE UP, JUST SURRENDER!

*"Now faith is the assurance of things hoped for,
the conviction of things not seen." -* **Hebrews 11:1**

B eing a parent is definitely not for the faint of heart. From birth, these little people are coloring our world with grocery store tantrums, boogers, poop-splosions, and various nerve-racking run-ins with the corners of, well, everything. As these little ones grow up, they'll begin to color their own world; discovering who they are, pursuing their own passions and chasing their dreams. You'll find yourself working to keep step with them; praying, guiding and influencing their every twist and turn; it's a dance that will sometimes make you feel like you have two left feet! I envision the transition of these stages of raising nations much like the process of teaching our kids to ride a bike. You hold on tight at first, making sure they understand everything about riding a bike. You give them detailed instructions, encouragement, and warnings about possible situations. Before you know it, you're running beside them as they take off on their own, with them eventually out riding your running pace, leaving you standing and looking on from the sidelines with cheers and encouragement as they take to the road before them. Yes, kids will fall off of the bike; yes, they will likely get banged up to some degree; yes, it's scary for them and for us, but in the midst of possible failure, we understand that the sooner we surrender control and trust that they'll use what we've taught them, the sooner they'll discover success. Like this simple bike-riding process, parenting is most enjoyable and exciting when we surrender control and rest in our role of stewardship.

Surrender is defined as giving yourself up, as into the power of another; to submit or yield.[4] Surrender is leaning not on your own understanding but finding God's strength in your weaknesses (**Proverbs 3:5**). Surrender is obeying God, even when you don't have the whole picture. Surrender is choosing to walk in faith instead of being led by fear. Surrender to God is the fruit of humility, operating through quiet trust.

> "BEHOLD, CHILDREN ARE A GIFT OF THE LORD, THE FRUIT OF THE WOMB IS A REWARD." **PSALM 127:3**

As Christian parents that are raising nations, we surrender ourselves to God in parenting because we understand, according to the Psalm above, that our children are a gift given to us by God. In fact, this Psalm says that our children are our reward; the Greek word for reward is *sakar* and it means payment of contract, compensation, or benefit. This word is the same word used in **Genesis 15:1** when God's words came to Abram in a vision saying, "DO NOT FEAR, ABRAM, I AM A SHIELD TO YOU; YOUR REWARD SHALL BE VERY GREAT." It's in the interaction with this vision that God promises a son to Abram. This Psalm reiterates to us that each child is a gift given to remind us of God's faithfulness in His promises; it's God revealing Himself to us over and over again through the face of a child, as a payment of the promise He made to Abram, which still produces fruit today. We surrender, because we understand that our children are not our property, they are a gift that was placed in our care and stewardship to remind the world that God keeps His word, and that He is our exceedingly great reward!

ABRAHAM'S SURRENDER

When Sarah gave birth to Isaac, she and Abraham experienced the fulfillment of the Lord's faithfulness. Up to this point, Abraham had believed that God was faithful, but now his faith met face to face with his experience. From the power of the manifestation of God's promise, Abraham would find the strength to face the total surrender God was going to ask of him.

> "Now it came about after these things, that God tested Abraham, and said to him, "Abraham!" and he said, "Here I am." He said, "Take now your son, your only son, whom you love, Isaac, and go to the land of Moriah, and offer him there as a burnt offering on one of the mountains of which I will tell you." So, Abraham rose early in the morning and saddled his donkey..." **Genesis 22:1-3a**

God had given Abraham a promise, a son through which his descendants would outnumber the stars (**Genesis 15:5**), and now God was asking Abraham to offer this promise up as a sacrifice back to God; to possibly end his life. Killing Isaac meant killing the promise of not just the present day, but the future that God had spoken through Isaac. This was an ultimate act of surrender and trust, which according to verse three, Abraham obeyed without argument. God did not command Abraham to commit this act of sacrifice, and then wink at him to let him know that He wasn't really going to make him go through with it, Abraham walked purely in faith, believing that God was good and faithful, and He would make it right. **Hebrews 11:19** says that Abraham "considered that God is able to raise

PEOPLE EVEN FROM THE DEAD, FROM WHICH HE ALSO RECEIVED HIM BACK AS A TYPE." Abraham was faced with a choice, to fear the threat of what could be, or to believe the goodness of God, and stand on the faith that God is able to perform what He promises no matter what (**Romans 4:21**). Abraham was being delivered of self: selfish desires, selfish motives, and selfish ideals regarding Isaac; was Abraham more in love with the promise or was he devoted in love to the One who gave him the promise? God was cultivating purity of heart in Abraham through his faith and surrender. Through surrender, Abraham had to accept that the bigger picture of Isaac's life was not about him, it was about what God was doing in and through him. As this story progresses in **Genesis 22:9-14**, we see that God intervened and provided a ram in the thicket, giving Isaac back to Abraham. This was a mark of two powerful events: Abraham experiencing God as his true provider, and the purification of the motive of Abraham's heart in stewardship over Isaac. Challenging times will test our underlying motives for our children's lives; will we stand in faith and trust God? Or will we give into the fear of natural possibilities and fight for control?

Do not fear the threat of the natural, believe the promise of the Spirit!

As I mentioned previously, I had our older daughter, Maiya, when I was a senior in high school. My husband, Justin, is not her biological father, yet he has raised her since she was two years old. We homeschooled Maiya through the sixth grade, and at ten years old, for a variety of reasons, her biological father requested that she start public school. Because Justin and I had full custody of her and had already been homeschooling her, we were not legally required to agree to the request of her biological father. However, we felt strongly that the Lord wanted us to let her go and trust Him with her life, which would also preserve our relationship with her long-term. This was a deeply difficult request of the Lord, since He was the one who impressed it upon us for me to be home and homeschool all of our children; it was the promise and the vision He had given us. It was just as difficult for our other two children because they had a close bond with their sister since they had spent every day with her for the past six years. It was a huge adjustment for our whole family, and it broke my heart into so many pieces. I remember laying on my bed in the fetal position, pregnant with David, sobbing my heart out to the Lord because I was so scared to let Maiya go; it felt like death to me. I remember how the Holy Spirit counseled my heart and reminded me of Abraham and how God provided a way when it seemed like there was no way. By every natural standard it didn't seem right to release our grasp on Maiya's life, but we knew God was asking us to do it for her sake and ours. So, we obeyed, and so He blessed. Those years were hard; letting go of a promise was hard, but God made all things work together for our good, we all flourished, and we were able to preserve a meaningful long-term connection with Maiya. Now we have the privilege of watching her become an incredible mama to her own daughter, and it's brilliantly redemptive!

There is a bigger picture for your child's future; God has given each one a destiny to fulfill, one that will impact their generation for the kingdom. Surrender requires us to view everything our nations go through from a heavenly perspective and trust God to work all things together for their good. Consistently surrendering your motives, desires, and self-will to God will cultivate a purity of trust and faith in who He is, and allows Him to show Himself as Jehovah Jireh, the Lord your Provider. When you spend time praying for your nations, I highly encourage you to first pray a prayer of surrender such as the one at the end of this chapter.

STEWARD OR SAVIOR

Surrender is knowing the difference between being your child's steward and being their savior. A steward is one who oversees or manages a person or possession, whereas a savior is one who rescues, delivers, or saves someone. God sent the only Savior there ever was or ever will be, Jesus Christ, so you can do yourself a favor, and get off the throne of your child's life, it doesn't fit you, nor was the role ever meant for you. Christ endured every hardship, bled every drop, and died a great death on a cross to fulfill His role as our Savior, and through Him and Him alone can we be saved, rescued, and delivered. This is great news!! The role God has entrusted to us over our nations is the role of a steward; one who oversees and manages with excellence what God has given us.

Stewarding your nations includes feeding, clothing, disciplining, instructing, equipping, praying for, schooling, and nurturing them. There are many decisions you will make within each element of stewardship; what kinds of food to feed them, how to educate them, and styles of discipline and instruction to use. These decisions are best made with prayerful consideration and will be unique to each family dynamic. Ultimately the line of stewardship is crossed into the savior role if our motive for the decisions we make are to somehow guarantee their rescue, deliverance, or salvation. For example: if I choose to homeschool my kids because I believe it's what God has asked me to do, I am stewarding my child's future according to the wisdom of God. I cross the line if my motive for homeschooling becomes an idol on which I lean to guarantee their future success, believing that it is the only way. No matter if God assigns my kids to be public schooled, private schooled, or homeschooled, their future success should rest on Christ and Christ alone. Likewise, I can choose to teach my children healthy living, but I cross the line if my motive for feeding (or restricting) certain foods is to guarantee their health and wellness, believing it's the only way. Specific foods, supplements, and exercises should not become an idol to which we look for a guarantee of our children's health, those things should simply be the method in which we partner with God to care for the body He's given our kids. We ultimately surrender to Him for sustained health and wellness. We approach spiritual stewardship the same; our motive for teaching our nations scripture, how to pray, and how to love God should be to act as an arrow pointing to Jesus which leads them to discover their personal relationship with Him. We cross the line when we think that raising them in our personal styles of devotion is the way to save them, or thinking the only way for them to have a relationship with Christ is if it's done our way. We cannot save our children we can only lead them to the One who saves, and what a privilege it is when we can fully embrace the power of partnership with God!

FEAR-BASED RAISING VS. LOVE-BASED RAISING.

> "THERE IS NO FEAR IN LOVE; BUT PERFECT LOVE CASTS OUT FEAR, BECAUSE FEAR INVOLVES PUNISHMENT, AND THE ONE WHO FEARS IS NOT PERFECTED IN LOVE." **1 JOHN 4:18**

When we are raising the children that God has given to us, we have two basic factors that will seek to drive our stewardship and parenting responses: love and fear. Love holds the faith to acknowledge that we are stewards, not saviors. Love (agapeo) is an operation of trust; it is a result of being perfected in the love of Christ; we cannot be love-based parents if we do not first receive the perfect love of Christ in our own life (**1 John 4:8**). When our stewardship is driven by love, we make choices in regard to our child's destiny out of the trust we have in God's faithfulness to fulfill that destiny. Love-based parenting operates in the *even ifs*, it believes the best in our kids' future, even when challenges arise, because we know that

God has the final word, and His word does not return to Him void. On the other hand, fear is performance-based; it is the response of seeing only punishment in circumstances. Fear-based parenting is hyper-focused on finding the right way instead of the right One, thus linking all outcomes to how well we perform in life. Fear is the typical response when we are not resting in love. When our parenting response is driven by fear, we will make decisions based on the innumerable *what ifs* that lurk around every corner.

I challenge you to start replacing your "what if" with "even if":

- What if my kid fails? → Even if my kid fails, I know God's plan does not!
- What if my kid gets sick? → Even if sickness comes, Jesus is the Healer!
- What if I make the wrong decision? → Even if I get it wrong God will make the crooked places straight!
- What if I look like a bad parent? → Even if others are against me, God is for me!

Fear says "What if" and Faith says "Even if!"

Love-based parenting searches for the treasure in every challenge and stands tall with confidence in Christ when the fire comes, while fear-based parenting finds the worst in every scenario, cowering at every small challenge, resorting to controlling, perfectionistic, manipulative, or overbearing behaviors. A love-based parent will embrace their weaknesses, boasting in the strength and power of Christ that is asserted through them, while the fear-based parent will dwell on their weaknesses, make excuses in their weaknesses, or deny that they have weaknesses all together. Love-based parenting sees opportunity for growth and lessons to be learned in failure, while fear-based parenting avoids any opportunity for failure, not wanting to lose any amount of control or order.

In the winter months of homeschooling my younger kids and I tend to frequent the public library on a weekly basis. When my second daughter, Evelyn, was eight years old, she asked me if she could have her own library card, because she really wanted to feel like a responsible young lady, and it would be cool to have a card with her name on it. I knew that this decision provided an opportunity for her to learn some lessons and grow through possible failure; losing books, forgetting to return them on time, etc. I explained to her that if she checked books out under her card, she would need to be responsible to keep track of them and their due dates, with the understanding that if any overdue fines were accrued on her account, that she would have to pay for them with her own money. She agreed to the terms and with a giant smile on her face, she excitedly signed her name on the card that the librarian handed to her. It wasn't more than a couple of months before her smile turned to a look of concern as her account reflected an overdue fine balance of $1.35. As we both looked at the screen for confirmation, I knew I had two options: either I embrace this opportunity for her to learn about deadlines, responsibility, and accountability by having her pay with her own money, or I bail her out, pay for it myself, and shut her card down for not paying close enough attention. I felt the Lord nudge me to let her learn the lesson, and so she opened her little pink purse with the embroidered flowers on it, and she pulled out one of only two crumpled dollar bills she had, along with a quarter and a dime. As she fed the money into the machine, I could see the reality of the lesson she was learning really hitting home. It was all I could do to not intervene with my own money, or at the very least, offer to replenish her little purse with the money she'd given up. I knew this lesson was important, and it would create a ripple effect for her future when she was paying serious bills and facing serious deadlines. She was sad for a bit about the money she had to surrender, but it created such a real lesson for her, that from that day on she kept a much closer eye on her borrowed library items, carefully returning them on time, or at least knowing what it would cost her if she didn't. Love-based parenting means we exercise faith and find small ways to let our kids fail, so that they are equipped with understanding through experience when it matters most. Don't let fear drive your decisions when you're raising your kids, you're only serving them a disservice and selling yourself short in the process. Have faith and give God the room to move in their life!

FEAR focuses on moving away from failure,
LOVE focuses on the faith to move towards destiny
despite the possibility of failure.

KILLING IDEALS WITHOUT KILLING VISION

God is a God of vision, dreams, and destiny. God wants us to take hold of the vision for not only our life but the lives of our nations. Often times, however, we mistake vision for ideals, and when we don't understand the difference between the two, it can tear at the fabric of our child's destiny and war against the will of God for their life. Vision is the ability to see or perceive; whether through prophetic insight, imagination, or anticipation. Vision is the foundation of faith as defined in **Hebrews 11:1** "NOW FAITH IS THE ASSURANCE OF THINGS HOPED FOR, THE CONVICTION OF THINGS NOT SEEN." When we have vision for our life or our kids' lives, we are standing in faith for the destiny that we see God has given them. An ideal, on the other hand, is essentially a standard or concept of perfection; when we look at our home, our marriage, our spiritual life, or the life and future of our nations, we may tend to have an ideal, a concept of perfection for those things. Whether we've seen it on social media, heard it on a podcast, or witnessed parts of it playing out in the lives of other families, we may have a place in our heart that drives towards this standard of what we want our life or our children's lives to look like in a perfect scenario. When we are led by parenting ideals, our children can quickly be seen as an inconvenience since they by nature are very unpredictable and unstable. I've unfortunately witnessed many parents who so wrestle with the ideals in their mind, that they throw themselves into very destructive patterns and cycles trying to attain this perfect image and standard, while driving themselves and their family insane. Vision will make you feel free, and excited, trusting in the plans that God has for today and the future. Vision will give you a sense of hopeful flexibility and an adventurous tenacity for cultivating relationships with your kids. Vision will give you rest when storms come, because you perceive the big picture of what God is doing in your life, and so you remain unmoved. Ideals will cause you to feel fearful, anxious, and overwhelmed because you have to constantly scramble to keep the pieces in place.

Some indications that lofty ideals are stealing from your family:

- There is more chaos than peace in your home.
- Small changes in the plans put you in a frazzle.
- You or your children are overwhelmed and commonly on the edge of tears.
- You wake up with dread, anticipating the daily maintenance ahead of you.
- You can only count on one hand, how many moments of joy-filled laughter you've had with your kids in the past few weeks.
- You and your spouse argue more than you dream together.
- You often feel like a failure or that you're not good enough.
- When you look at your children, you often see what you'd like to change.

If you are experiencing one or more of these scenarios, it's okay, don't fear! God loves you enough to meet you where you are, and take you where you need to be, so that you and your children will walk in freedom and peace. Write down any areas where you feel your ideals have swallowed you and your family up, and then repent of any behaviors or mindsets you've operated in. Ask God to replace these concepts of perfection with His vision and destiny for your life, marriage, household, and the lives of your children. As you go about your days, learn to recognize when ideals begin to sneak in and steal, immediately call them out, submit them to God, resist the ideology and walk in freedom!

> "SUBMIT TO GOD, THEREFORE, RESIST THE DEVIL AND HE WILL FLEE FROM YOU." **JAMES 4:7**

Surrender means that we must view everything with a heavenly perspective and ask ourselves, *"how does this affect the big picture?"* As you surrender, choose your battles, let go of things that don't add any value to the vision, pray for your children without ceasing, engage in spiritual warfare and intercession on their behalf, and be led by the Spirit when you respond and instruct, and you will find more adventure and purpose in your parenting than ever before!

Submit + Resist = Freedom!

DON'T GIVE UP - SURRENDER!

God's grace is so powerful and perfect when you are surrendered to Him, His strength truly shines in your weaknesses so embrace your lack; you can do this thing called raising nations! Don't give up on the assignment God has given you, instead, be encouraged that He hand-picked you to raise these leaders. It isn't easy, but it's reward-ing and life changing. I encourage you to give up the striving to have it all under control, give up the need to have everything fit in a nice box, give up the fight to be super-parent and do it all, give up the stubbornness, pride, and fear, but don't give up the mission to stew-ard your kids with the heart of God. Trust God, He loves your kids more than you ever could. When you find yourself wanting to give up, fall to your knees and surrender to God instead!

PRAYER

Father, I thank you for the gift of these children, I acknowledge and accept that I am not their savior, but I have been given stewardship over their earthly lives. Thank you for loving each child immeasurably more than I ever could. I give them over to You for your purpose and plan and I receive them back to build them up in their destiny. Strip any selfish way or wrong motive within me, so that they can be everything You've destined them to be. Thank you that in surrender, you will give me rest and enjoyment as I raise them to be tomorrow's kingdom warriors, in Jesus' name, Amen!

REFLECTION/DISCUSSION QUESTIONS:

1. What areas do you need to surrender to the Lord?

2. Where have you operated in fear instead of faith?

CHAPTER 5

INTENTIONALITY

"Nobody finished well by accident"
—John C. Maxwell

S everal years ago, after our fourth baby, my husband and I decided to embark on the adventure of a short-course triathlon together. This particular course we were completing included a quarter-mile swim, followed immediately by a ten-mile bike ride, and then a three-mile run to the finish line. We had signed up in March and had to be ready to compete by the end of July, giving us a window of about four months to train. We had no previous experience with this type of competition and were clueless as to what to expect, so we asked around for wisdom from those who'd gone before us. We gathered enough information to be able to put together a basic training plan, which started off with running two or three miles three times per week and going for a ten-mile bike ride a couple of times per week, while being careful to monitor our nutrition. Once the ice was off of the lake in town and we were able to jump in the water, we began to swim short lengths, working our way up to the quarter-mile distance required for the short course. Beyond training for each individual leg of the race, we also had to practice transitioning from one leg to the next:

swimming to biking and then biking to running. To train for the total sequence we would swim a quarter mile, hop on our bikes and ride around the lake twice and then immediately jump off to run 3 miles. It was insanely hard the first couple of times, and it often felt like my legs were going to fall off, but my husband and I diligently trained every week. I cannot say that at any point I ever felt like an expert, or even an excellent swimmer, runner, or biker, however I felt confident enough in each activity, I'd trained as well as I could, and I felt I would be able to carry myself through to the end.

"Under pressure, you don't rise to the occasion, you sink to the level of your training. That's why we train so hard."
– anonymous Navy Seal

When race day came, I was nervous but confident, knowing I had done the best I could to train and prepare for the challenge ahead of me. When the gun went off, I jumped in the water ready to tackle the first leg of the race. Immediately my excitement gave way to panic when my goggles fogged up and I could no longer see anything. In addition to that, the seaweed that had surfaced from the previous night's storm wrapped around my ankles as a scream simultaneously rang out from a woman who, in giving way to her panic, was clinging to a large buoy in the water. My imagination ran wild over all the possible ways I could drown, and I realized the only thing I had to lean on was the intentionality of my training. I thought about giving up all my hard work and heading back, but I didn't, instead I focused on my training, determined to finish what I had worked so hard for. As I exited the water from the quarter-mile swim, thankful to be alive, I slipped my wet, sandy feet into my shoes and hopped on my bike, riding for ten miles up and down hill. Jumping off of my bike, my legs wobbled, and I felt them collapsing under me, but I did my best to coerce them to run anyway. It felt reminiscent of a dream where you're being chased, and you want to run but your legs are glued to the ground, getting you nowhere. I stopped to stretch, wondering if I should just walk the rest of the way and give up, but I leaned into my training. *"You've done this five times before in training, you can do this now"* I told myself. Capping the race off with the full three-mile run, I finally crossed the finish line, and I wasn't even the last one! I laid on the ground and decided I'd likely never do that again. Although the process was tumultuous and my performance not pretty, my husband and I crossed the finish line and celebrated our victory together, knowing we'd done our best and finished strong. Intentionality drove our determination to achieve the vision we had for completing this triathlon.

Simply put, intentionality is having an aim and doing something with a purpose; it's determining the target for the arrows you release in life. Intentionality is making a play in the game instead of sitting on the sidelines observing. Intentionality is mapping a course, zeroing in, and having a focus. Intentionality does not equal perfection, because no matter how hard we plan, we will have variables unaccounted for and moments of failure; but with intentionality we can fail with purpose and use failure to recalibrate our aim. Passivity allows life to happen to you, intentionality causes you to be led by the Spirit and be driven by destiny in all that you do.

I see parenting in this same light; the goal is not perfection, but intentionality. When we cross the finish line and stand accountable before God at the end of our life, we can stand knowing that, though our process may not have been perfect and we may have considered giving up, we pressed on and raised our nations with a heart of intentionality using our resources to the best of our capability. Being an intentional steward of your nations means that you have purpose in all that you do; not letting precious resources of time, money, and relationship slip through your fingers. Take intentional time to be spiritually discerning and ask hard questions in prayer such as, *"What does my child need from me?" "How can I love better?" "Where do I lack wisdom and need to ask God for it?"*. Instead of falling apart in a crisis, the intentional parent sees opportunity for them and their nations to learn and grow.

---

*Intentionality will cause you to see the opportunities
in every challenge.*

WHAT IS YOUR "WHY"?

Intentionality is essentially driven by your "why". Your "why" is your grounding wire because parenting can often cause you to feel completely out of control and uncertain if you are doing the right thing or making any difference at all. You need to have a point of grounding that reminds you during adversity why you have been trusted to steward your children and why you're on the course you've set.

The "why" of raising kids is really two-fold, the kingdom view, and the frontline view. The kingdom "why" is the greater purpose; the big picture; the mission of spiritual multiplication. As a kingdom-minded parent you will ask big picture questions, *"What purpose am I helping my children cultivate?"* or *"Why does intentionality and accountability matter long-term?"* The answers to these kingdom questions are that we are raising Christ-centered nations to pick up where we leave off (**2 Timothy 1:6**), to bring light into darkness, to set the captives free, to bind the broken-hearted and bring salvation to the lost (**Isaiah 61**). Therefore, in order for them to effectively take on this mission when they are older, they must first learn the character and heart of Christ-likeness, which is where the frontline "why" comes in.

*"Train up a child in the way he should go, even when he is old, he will not depart from it." - **Proverbs 22:6***

The frontline "why" is the mission behind our everyday actions as a parent; the fruit of every arrow that we shoot, every word we speak, every decision we make, every step we take. On the frontlines is where the battles are fought and won, and so the fruit of our frontline actions will fulfill the greater kingdom mission. Possible frontline questions you will ask are, *"Why do I limit screen time?"*, to protect their mind, and teach them self-control. *"Why am I disciplining them for their actions?"*, to teach integrity and accountability. *"Why do we take them to church every Sunday, even when they don't want to go?"*, to teach them the value of the nation they are a part of. *"Why do I keep an atmosphere of worship in the home?"*, to model love for the presence of God. In essence, our frontline "why" will drive and fulfill the kingdom "why" by cultivating the heart of Christ in our children and pointing them to a relationship with Him.

- "Why do we discipline our children?" – **Proverbs 12:1, 13:24**
- "Why do we teach our kids to forgive?" – **Luke 6:37**
- "Why do we teach our kids to love others?" – **1 John 4 & 1 Corinthians 13**
- "Why do we teach our kids to give generously?" – **2 Corinthians 9:6-8**
- "Why is admitting wrong and apologizing important?" – **James 4:6**

The foundation of your "why" will be found in scripture, and the manifestation of your "why" will be unique to each family and must be sought in prayer and spiritual discernment. For example, God is interested in every child knowing and serving Christ, yet on one hand He may lead one family to homeschool in order to fulfill this mission, and on the other hand He may lead your neighbor to send their kids to a private or public school for their own unique reasons to accomplish the same mission of knowing and serving Christ. It does not make homeschool, private school, or public school better or worse than the others, it simply makes it unique to the needs of your kids and your family. It matters not so much the vehicle that takes you, but the focus of the destination that you seek. God knows what's best for you, your kids, and your family and it will change with different seasons of life; so, seek Him continually for new and fresh strategies to raise your kids with intention, purpose, and efficiency.

> "LET US NOT GROW WEARY OF WELL DOING, FOR IN DUE SEASON WE WILL REAP A HARVEST IF WE DO NOT GIVE UP." - **GALATIANS 6:9**

Intentionality will keep you on track in the challenging seasons. The greatest "why" of parenting you'll ever ask is, *"Why did God give me my children?"* Remember in the previous chapter that one of the main reasons God gives us children is to serve as a daily reminder of His faithfulness to His promises, so let that foundational "why" encourage your heart and be your grounding wire when challenging times come. When you feel like things are falling apart or you just cannot go on, going back to your "why" to remember what your intentions are in raising your nations will turn you right side up.

THE BUTTERFLY EFFECT

Do you ever wonder if your actions today really matter for tomorrow? Back in 1963 a mathematician by the name of Edward Lorenz published a theoretical study on the effects of a single action and how its ripple effect changes future events. He used the Butterfly as an example:

The idea that a butterfly's wings might create tiny changes in the atmosphere that may ultimately alter the path of a tornado or delay, accelerate or even prevent the occurrence of a tornado in another location. The butterfly does not power or directly create the tornado but is intended to imply that the flap of the butterfly's wings can cause the tornado: in the sense that the flap of the wings is a part of the initial conditions. [5]

This concept—that a gentle flap of a butterfly's wings could set something so foundational into motion that it has the potential to alter weather patterns weeks later—was preposterous and laughable to the New York Science Academy. Lorenz's theory was shelved and used as science-fiction material for many fictional movies and books. Some thirty years after his initial theory was published, scientists began to realize it's validity through various experiments, eventually adopting it into the scientific realm as "The Law of Sensitive Dependence Upon Initial Conditions."   This scientific concept that even the smallest actions today can have staggering effects in the future is not limited to weather patterns and nature, it can be applied physically, spiritually, mentally, and relationally. Simply put, what you do today can be felt tomorrow.

The Butterfly Effect is just as powerful in the negative as it is in the positive expression of raising nations, there are many phrases that were said to me as a child that stuck with me and rippled all the way to adulthood; good and bad. Whether my mom said, *"get out of my sight, I can't stand you!"* or *"I'm proud of you."*, I heard it loud and clear, and it rippled. Small and seemingly unimportant moments of my life as a child impacted me as a woman; I remember at ten years old my dad letting me buy a grocery bag full of ingredients and gave me full reign of the kitchen to create a masterpiece cake. He sat from his chair in the living room cheering me on… it flopped, but I remember how his confidence in my ability to learn caused me to believe I could do hard things. In the same way I remember being left at home alone as a young fourteen-year-old for days with no food, no money, no phone, and no transportation while my dad was succumbing to addiction. Those weeks imbedded a belief that life was about survival and there wasn't room for childhood, let alone childlikeness. It rippled. I thank God that He was more than able to redeem time, renew my mind, and reconcile my hurts regardless of the ripple, that's just how good He is!

> "DO NOT BE DECEIVED, GOD IS NOT MOCKED; FOR WHATEVER A MAN SOWS, THIS HE WILL ALSO REAP." **- GALATIANS 6:7**

Your children are your number one mission field. There is no greater assignment in a parent's life than to raise tomorrow's leaders. Yes, there will be other assignments that God invites you into while you raise your nations, but never underestimate the power of this abrupt season in life when you pour into the future of who God has destined your children to be. It's such a privilege to come along side of these little people and speak life into them, shape them, train them, and love them into their destiny. When we take time to be intentional and consider the effects of what we say and do, not just for today, but for tomorrow as well, we have the ability to encourage or hinder the way our children will see the world and God when they are older. They will make decisions as adults based off of the perspective that was instilled in them as young people. What you do today will matter in your children's lives tomorrow, so take a minute before you act to be sure you want them to harvest the fruit of your words and actions when they grow up. Whatever seeds you sow, you will also reap in relationship with them later. Remember that Jesus is able to redeem, renew and reconcile so if and *when* you mess up, take it to Him quickly, He's good at what He does!

What does it look like to become an intentional parent? We will each need to answer this question for ourselves as we commune with God and capture His heart for our family. God has challenged me personally to have more of a direct and intentional investment in my nations by being present, keeping healthy margins, and prioritizing passions.

BE PRESENT

There is a difference between parenting and raising kids; *parenting* your children will demand your physical and mental presence in their lives, and *raising* your children will require spiritual and emotional presence on top of that. Parenting children directly relates to the immediate vision for their lives: survival. Just getting through the day, keeping the kids alive and healthy both physically and mentally can sometimes prove to be a challenge. So often after feeding them, washing them, educating them, providing for their needs, and keeping them safe from harm, we can be tempted to stop and call it good. It is good. It's good to be a physically present parent to your children, it's an important part of the job, but it's only a portion of your role to them.

"Wherever you are, be all there."- ***Jim Elliot***

Raising children directly addresses the big picture vision: thriving. Investing in your children spiritually, emotionally, and relationally will build a quality of life that will cause them to thrive internally. Raising children requires sacrifice because it means moving beyond how you feel in the moment, and giving your internal as well as your external focus to what is going on in their lives beyond the superficial. There is a plethora of ways to invest time and resources into raising your children by stewarding their heart, let's dive into just a few.

- **Schedule dates to be with your kids** – Ask your kids a simple question; *"What brings you life?"* Do they like to go on walks, go for ice cream, or go to the park? If your child prefers to be quiet and read, take them to a library or coffee shop, don't bring them to an amusement park. If you are more of an introvert and your child is very social, you'll probably need to stretch yourself to take them to do things that bring them life, which may include noisy, crowded, and out-of-your-comfort-zone type of scenarios. When you take the time and effort to experience their world their way, it shows them that you have vested interest in more than just your own enjoyment. God invested in us by sending His Son into our situation to experience the good and bad right along with us so that He could be the kind of Savior that could understand what we are going through (**Hebrews 4:15**). Your children will remember that you came into their experiences and took the time to understand the lens through which they see life.

- **Schedule dates for your kids to be with you** – At first glance this may seem redundant, but it's not. In addition to stepping in to experience your child's world, I encourage you to extend an invitation for them to come along with you, and step into your world. What brings *you* life? Do you like to play games, put puzzles together, watch movies? Do you like to build things, work on cars, or shop? Whatever it is that you enjoy, set up some time to invite your kids to participate with you. Teach them about the activity, what you love and why you enjoy it. Include them in your happiness. God extends His invitation to us as His children to step into His heart when He gives us opportunities to serve and love others. When we partner with Christ in ministry, God is showing us His heart and trusting us with His world.

- **Unplug and just be** – Put away your phone and devices and fix your thoughts on your surroundings. Be present in your tasks with your kids; bath time, homework, mealtime etc. What are your kids saying to you? Ask good questions. Look into their eyes and let God show you how He sees them. Make a mental note of what you love about them as you watch them play and interact with the world around them. Let them see you just "be" instead of always "do". God calls us in this way to "BE STILL AND KNOW THAT I AM GOD" **(Psalm 46:10)** because He knows that in the quietness of our heart, without all the striving of life, His voice will supersede all anxiety, worry, fear, or stress and bring clarity to our true purpose here on earth; to love and be loved. When you make yourself available to absorb all that God has for you with your children, it shows them that they are loved, and how to love.

"To a child, love is spelled T-I-M-E" – **Zig Ziglar**

- **Family Devotions** – The phrase *"family devotions"* tends to bring one's imagination to a picture of a pressed family sitting tall and poised around the kitchen table, well dressed, and listening respectfully while one person reads aloud, immediately followed by organized conversation and polished prayers. I spent years feeling like we failed at devotions because our times were rarely ever picturesque. The reality for our family has been that at one time or another, when we're gathered together, there is bedhead, loud noise, interruptions, crying, farting, spilled milk, fighting, and whining. Instead of respectful listening, there are times when we spend most of our energy re-directing and correcting behavior. Regardless of the often unpolished nature of our gatherings, some of our greatest spiritual conversations as a family have come during our time of devotions; the time of day when we sit together and focus on Christ through prayer, reading, and sharing. There is no right or wrong way to do family devotions. There may be times when you'll want to read from a devotional book together to get the conversation started, other times you may find yourself simply reading a scripture together and digging further into its meaning and provision. We even have seasons when we use question prompts from the conversation cards over dinner. Carving out a little time each day or a few times a week to gather your family, read the scriptures out loud together, share devotional stories, pray together, and talk about what Jesus has done and is doing in your family's lives places value and priority on spiritual growth. It also creates good habits for your children for years to come. The goal is presence, not perfection.

- **Eat Together** – Studies have shown that although less than 50% of American families eat dinner together more than 3 times per week, almost 90% of families have a desire to do so, and rightfully so since there are so many incredible scientific benefits to sharing meals together. Some of the most common benefits to sharing at least one meal each day as a family include your child having a higher self-esteem, a lower likelihood of drug use, lower possibility for depression and anxiety, stronger sense of identity, and higher academic performance[6]. Perhaps you have a unique schedule like my family does, and dinner meals may not always be ideal to share together. My husband and I and our four young children ate dinner almost every night together for the first ten years of our marriage. Then his career took a very different direction, resulting in him being home more in the mornings and less in the evenings. Since we homeschool, we were able to be flexible and decided to be intentional about sharing breakfast together each morning before he would head out. As our children grew to teenagers and young adults, our season allowed for us to have intentional dinner time together just two or three times per week. Whether it's breakfast, lunch, or dinner that works for you, have a goal to eat at least one meal together each day, at the dinner table, with no screens. Once you have established the meal that you will purpose to share each day, make it a quality time to be together. Play a quick card game or board game just before or after you eat. You could also write down some intentional questions to ask each other; a great tool that our family has used to get the conversation going is something called the "Chat Pack". These packs have over a hundred different fun questions to ask and they come in a variety of categories. You can purchase them on www.thequestionguys.com. Share, laugh and connect!!

KEEP HEALTHY MARGINS

If you want to know the God you serve, look at your calendar. We live in a time when there are more activities, events, sports and extracurricular options than ever before. There is so much pressure to participate and experience everything that comes our way, it's no wonder that anxiety has increased so much that is has been declared the most common mental illness in the United States, effecting around 40 million adults[7]. Keeping healthy margins means allowing ample time beyond what is necessary for any given activity in your day, including errands, appointments, work, school, or sports. Margins leave room for teaching moments and maturity, along with opportunities for enjoying your everyday life. It isn't healthy for your mental, emotional, or relational state of being to be packed to the gills day after day with random stuff to do; just because there is time in a day doesn't mean it needs to be filled with activity or work. Remember, we are not just parenting our children from a natural standpoint, but more importantly we are raising our nations to be Godly men and women, therefore, we must prioritize healthy margins that allow for intentional spiritual growth and teaching them to fall in love with their Creator. If we are constantly running around, busy, absent, tasking, yelling or exhausted, what kind of example of worship are we leading them in?

Leaving generous margins of time throughout your days and weeks will create space to be relaxed and at peace with your schedule. Margins allow for presence over perfection; if you have ample space for hiccups or delays in your day, you are less likely to feel pressured into perfection, instead, you'll be allowed the space for problem solving. Keeping healthy margins means you can be present in the simple act of living and raising your nations.

- **Room to Breathe** – Be careful not to over pack your days with constant appointment-running and activity, spread it out and leave room to breathe. Keeping margins around the activities and appointments in each day gives you the room to make memories while you live out your daily commitments. More margin means less rushing, stress, and anxiety for you and your kids, especially your kids who are a bit slower paced or more introverted.

- **Flex Your "No" Muscle** – Take control of what you say yes to and what you say no to. Just because it can be done, doesn't mean it should be done. Each family will have to decide what is a "yes" and what is a "no" for their family in the current season, and we are all different. Just because you can cook and there is a meal train that was emailed to you, doesn't mean you have to say yes. Just because there are needs doesn't mean you can fill them all; even good things in wrong seasons aren't right things! One of the many ways my husband and I personally decided to create boundaries is by limiting our children to one sport per season because it is too demanding for our family to be running around day after day, sometimes several times a day, sitting at sporting practices and events. Whatever it is in your schedule that is robbing you of peace and time for closeness as a family, get rid of it, it's truly not worth the consequences you'll face later.

> *Even right things in wrong seasons become hinderances of success.*

- **Keep a "Sabbath"** – Choose a day of the week and even multiple weeks of the year to keep clear from any scheduled commitments or appointments, putting away devices and even housework. This will allow for rest, recuperation, and family connection along with the flexibility to be spontaneous together. We like to use Sundays as a day of rest from work and schedules, we usually float in the pool, go out to eat, watch a movie, or put a puzzle together. Additionally, Justin and I will often take off a week in the fall, over Christmas, and then a week in the spring and summer. These weeks we take time to find fun things to do together, get some projects done on our property, and enjoy a slower paced connection with the family. Maybe this particular rhythm isn't possible for you personally, it's just an example of how we take sabbaths throughout the year, but however you decide, being intentional to save days and weeks to unplug from the hustle and just be with your family will give you refreshment and grounding.

"Efforts and courage are not enough without purpose and direction" — **John F. Kennedy**

PRIORITIZING PASSIONS

We have four amazing children; we had our two girls first then our two boys, and the age span between our oldest and youngest is 10 years. From the chapters you've read so far, I hope it's clear to see that we have always had the vision to seek and prioritize the kingdom and raising our family for Jesus, which includes carefully managing our time together. From the time of starting our family, Justin and I had decided that we wanted our kids to get ample physical activity and learn the lessons of being on a team, but we didn't want to allow sports and activities to rule our lives and take away from the mission of raising our nations with kingdom focus. It seemed easy to rightly divide when they were little. We signed them up for things like community t-ball, soccer, and basketball and Justin would often get involved and coach. Our girls were not seriously interested in physical sports, they were more interested in engaging with creative activities or learning about animals and babysitting, so we easily kept our family's mission regarding extra-curricular activities on track for the first 17 years of parenting. However, once our boys started entering the age of getting serious about sports things shifted for us. Basketball was the sport that became a passion for both of them and, as most parents in the sports world know, sports are much different than they were twenty years ago. The time commitment and demand for every ounce of a player's attention and energy is absolutely insane—every child is to engage as if they are going pro.

The tension we find ourselves in as parents is that we want to protect our family rhythms, but we also see the value in encouraging our kids to pursue their passions. Justin and I wanted our nations to learn the discipline of practice, team effort, commitment, and failing forward and for us it seemed sports could offer a great environment to learn such disciplines. So, we prayed for God to help us navigate the mission of our family as we included this new piece to the puzzle. When you give God the right to direct your life, He will help you pull it off well! We leaned into intentionality and decided that we would participate as a family; going to games and tournaments together and finding ways to keep our connection as we supported the boys. We had to get intentional and creative with mealtimes, which meant we would wait to eat later when practice was over so we could connect, or we would go out for a meal together after the game. We've been adamant about minimizing activities and sports to one per season, as well as finding teams to play on that are competitive but less demanding. There have been times we've refused practices over holidays or stayed back from two-week, out of state tournaments that placed too much of a stress on our family's time and finances. It has not been easy to get the side-eye from other parents or have to console one of our kids because they had to miss out, but it has been a powerful season of actively training our nations to prioritize their passions correctly while keeping their focus on kingdom pursuit. This may mean they cannot be the star players, but they can still give 100% effort and be a star human being. In spite of the boundaries we've fought for, both of our boys have been on the starting JV and Varsity teams and have exceled to their best, all while keeping the main thing the main thing. When we raise our children with careful intentionality, we are not necessarily guaranteeing them a perfect life, but a solid foundation of integrity, along with a great potential for success as they learn and grow.

PRAYER

Jesus, thank you that you are an intentional Savior! Thank you for living your life with the intention to redeem your people both today, tomorrow, and forever. God, would you instill in me a heart that seeks intentional opportunity to invest in my family? Would you give me vision to see with intentionality, and to listen with an inclined ear to Your voice in the midst of many voices? Holy Spirit, would you guide me in each moment to throw off things that don't matter and embrace the valuable treasures in each day? Help me become one that creates margin, rests in the sabbath of Jesus, keeps the main thing the main thing, and seeks secret treasure in hidden places. I pray this in Jesus' name, AMEN!

REFLECTION/DISCUSSION QUESTIONS:

1. What areas have you been successful with intentionality?

2. What areas would you like to lay at the Lord's feet and receive grace to become more intentional?

3. What distractions might you need to give up in order to become successful with intentionality?

CHAPTER 6

CULTIVATING KINGDOM CULTURE

*"Seek first the Kingdom of God and His righteousness,
and all these things will be added to you." –* **Matthew 6:33**

I t was 7pm, still no dinner, and I was starving. We had been invited to my good friend's daughter's Quinceanera; a Latin coming-of-age party for girls turning fifteen. We had dressed up a little, hopped in the car, and with four small children in tow we got to the venue early assuming it would be very similar to an ordinary birthday party–you show up, you eat, you visit for a bit, and then you leave. With this expectation, we naturally held the kids off from snacking beforehand, re-assuring them that there would be plenty of food at the party! I scanned the room but didn't see my friend or her daughter, and since we didn't know anyone else at this party, we took our seats at a table and waited for them to show up. We had been sitting at the table for about an hour when it dawned on me that this was not your average birthday party. The people continued to arrive dressed in black tie suits, evening gowns, settling into their sparkling beverages, completely unbothered that it was after 7pm and still no birthday girl to be seen or dinner to be eaten. They laughed and visited as if this were the normal rhythm for this type of gathering. I leaned to the guest sitting a little further down and asked a bit about how a Quinceanera is celebrated. This guest explained that it's actually more like a wedding, including gorgeous gowns, professional pictures, sitdown style meals, speeches, and of course a grand entrance with special dances happening BEFORE dinner! Since there was still no birthday girl, I understood that we were a long way from feeding our hungry and restless children… It was over the rumbling of my own stomach that I realized how ill prepared our expectations were and just how different cultures can be.

Fast forward many years later, we found ourselves hosting a coming-of-age party for our older daughter, Maiya, and five years after that our younger daughter, Evelyn. Coming of age parties in traditional American culture are typically called the "Sweet 16" party. Maiya's Sweet 16 was a surprise party in a private bowling lounge with a variety of desserts, drinks, and friends, while Evelyn's party was at the lake, open-house style with a taco bar, fun music, summer dresses, and pink/gold/white decorations – Aikin to more of a graduation party. Justin and I had to chuckle as we put those parties together thinking back to our hangry children and our rumbling stomachs at 7pm, being reminded that whether it's a Quinceanera, Sweet 16, or a Bat mitzvah, our children will all come of age and each culture has a unique way of celebrating those moments. If you're wondering about the rest of the Quinceanera story, the birthday girl was delayed for various reasons and tradition was that there was dancing and pictures before dinner, so we didn't end up eating anything until almost 8pm…4 hours after we arrived. I'll let you imagine how that went with four small children and a hangry mama! Good times, good times.

Culture is said to be the lifeblood of a vibrant society, it points us in the direction of how to remember the past, live in the present, and dream for the future. Biblically speaking the concept of culture is discussed throughout both the Old and New testaments, with the Old Testament focused mainly on the outward culture of God's people and humanity itself, while the New Testament reveals the inner culture of the Kingdom through Christ. My intention is not to write an entire chapter on the statistics of culture, but to start the discussion on what kingdom culture is and how we cultivate it in our hearts and in our home as we share it with the world around us.

To know kingdom culture is to first know the King, Jesus. **Luke 17:21** records Jesus' words, "FOR INDEED THE KINGDOM OF GOD IS WITHIN YOU." The kingdom is not about external labor, it's an internal surrender. If the kingdom is internal, then what has been placed inside of us that is functioning as the kingdom? **Colossians 1:27** reveals that "CHRIST IN YOU IS THE HOPE OF GLORY" Paul's letter to the Corinthians confirms this, that our "BODY IS THE TEMPLE OF THE HOLY SPIRIT" **- 1 Corinthians 6:19-20**. Jesus is the King; kingdom culture is found in who He is, and it lives in us when we receive Him. To know the character and lordship of Jesus in our personal life produces fruit in our hearts and is then activated in our homes.

You'll notice that this chapter is specifically and purposefully not titled "*Creating* Kingdom Culture". There is a stark difference between cultivating and creating. To cultivate indicates that you are promoting the growth of something that *already* exists, whereas creating something would imply that you have to bring into being that which does not already exist. Often times we can become convinced that having kingdom culture in our home is simply an outward appearance to achieve; the act of having family devotions, speaking kind words, daily prayer time, and scripture memorization. While those things will be the fruit born to a household rooted in kingdom culture, it does not define the value of the kingdom as Paul said, "THE KINGDOM OF GOD IS NOT MEAT AND DRINK..." - **Romans 14:17**. To cultivate kingdom culture, it first has to exist *in* you, then you will promote the growth of it in your household by letting it live *through* you, furthermore finding that "THE KINGDOM OF HEAVEN IS AT HAND" - **Matthew 4:17**. If you approach kingdom culture in the home by setting a bunch of outward rules, regulations, and guidelines, you'll be met with disappointment and frustration time and time again. This will also breed the fruit of hypocrisy–outward cleanliness with an inward disturbance, and your kids will sniff it out the moment they come of an age that they can discern the difference. For example, if you preach about receiving the kingdom like a child with wonder and awe, yet you are crusty, rigid, and critical, they will likely reject your attempts. If you preach generosity as an attribute of the kingdom, yet you're stingy, you obsess over money (whether having it or not having it) and you speak with a poverty mindset, they may become confused and suspicious. Another important thing to note is that while your nations are young, you are the primary source of cultivating the culture in your home, but as those little ones grow older, it's advantageous for you to allow space for them to contribute to the culture as well. Inevitably our teens will contribute something to the household culture whether we like it or not so, it behooves us to model how to receive the kingdom for themselves, live it out, and continue to promote the fruit of it in the home.

Now that we understand that Jesus is the King, and His life was the ultimate example of the kingdom, let's explore a couple of the attributes of His life and how He taught the kingdom in the scriptures. After we explore these attributes together, I pray that you'll be inspired to open the scriptures and keep the discovery and adventure going for yourself!

FORM FOLLOWS FUNCTION

> "AND HE WAS SAYING, 'HOW SHALL WE PICTURE THE KING-
> DOM OF GOD, OR BY WHAT PARABLE SHALL WE PRESENT IT?
> IT IS LIKE A MUSTARD SEED, WHICH, WHEN SOWN UPON THE
> SOIL, THOUGH IT IS THE SMALLEST OF ALL THE SEEDS THAT
> ARE UPON THE SOIL, YET WHEN IT IS SOWN, IT GROWS UP AND
> BECOMES LARGER THAN ALL THE GARDEN PLANTS, AND FORMS
> LARGE BRANCHES, WITH THE RESULT THAT THE BIRDS OF THE
> SKY CAN NEST UNDER ITS SHADE.'" – **MARK 40:30-32**

The smallest of all the seeds… 2000 years ago, a baby was born to a young virgin of no prestigious family name or fortune. He was born in a barn under the humblest of circumstances. This baby had come with the kingdom government upon His shoulders, to serve His own and save the world; this would be the One they had waited for. You and I have the privilege of beholding the birth of Christ, as we celebrate it each year knowing the power that it held and still holds. However, the Jewish people at that time would experience a vastly different viewpoint. They would miss the impact of their King as they sought the largest of the trees, not the smallest of all the seeds. This parable of the mustard seed is a simile that describes the humble function of the kingdom being sown into the soil of our hearts, growing into a form of provision for the world around us. Jesus comes to us in mustard seed form and invites us into a process of discovering the kingdom function in our lives, the fruit of "what it looks like" subsequently then takes shape. This concept is what is commonly known as, "Form Follows Function".

Form Follows Function was originally a 19th century architectural design principle, later adopted by many as art theory. The concept implies that it's important to first understand the function, or purpose for which something exists, and then to let the form, or appearance, follow it; in other words, to shape the appearance of a thing according to its purpose. For example, if I were to design a chair, I would first need to know what kind of function this chair would have; is it for sitting at a dining table? Perhaps it's for relaxing or taking to the beach? Once I establish the function of the chair then I can design a form to support the function. One of the most central kingdom attributes that we have cultivated in our nations is to understand that what is most important is not their performance for God, but their purpose in God. Justin and I have spent countless years having conversations around identity, purpose, and how God has uniquely wired each family member to contribute to the overall plan in the earth. We have prayed and helped our kids excavate their uniqueness using the **Romans 12** Grace Gifts; when we would see Evelyn leading a group of younger kids, we'd call out the leader in her; when Matthew would come and ask what he can do to help (as he often did), we would edify the serving gift he possesses. When we help them discover their unique functional approach to life it opens their eyes to what it might look like to contribute to the world around them. As our littles have turned into teenagers, those aching questions about what they will do with their lives continues to yield to who they are in Christ and how He wants to partner with them in their assignments. It's not so important to worry about what life is supposed to look like, but how we show up with Him each day. In my opinion, it's possibly the most significant, fruit-bearing kingdom attribute we've cultivated in our home. Form follows function is a lens we encourage our children to see life through, it's also a lens we can use to see our children and their process.

Our older son, Matthew, tends to have a more steady, rational personality; he doesn't have big emotions necessarily, but he has an intense desire for justice and honor. His thought process is deep and intense, and when he processes, he does so verbally. He often voices every pitstop along the way as his heart reaches for understanding, finally arriving at the destination of resolve. If you happen to be a part of an equation involving this process, you may hear things that will tempt you to be offended if you don't have the grit to hear the heart behind the words. One particular occasion when he was entering the season of increased hormones and his processing seemed back-to-back every day, him and I got into a heated discussion over who-knows-what. He said a few things that my heart leapt at the opportunity to be offended by, and I was not in the mood to put my wounded feelings in their rightful place. I was gearing up for my lecture on respect and gratefulness when the Holy Spirit interrupted my thoughts with a challenge to ask him some thoughtful questions. As I sat down with him and gave him space to process, he began to share with me his heart for justice, how he feels a pull to know God more but doesn't know how, and how he wants to hear God's voice. I realized in that moment that this 12-year-old was encountering the function of the Spirit drawing him near and he wasn't sure what to do with it, so he interpreted it as anger and discontentedness. After listening to his heart and affirming the value of his feelings, I discussed the importance of communicating clearly and respectfully, appealing to his desire for honor. If I would have put a larger focus on fixing the *form* of his attitude, I would have missed the *function* of his heart and the opportunity to train him would have passed me by.

As we cultivate kingdom culture in our homes, our aim is not what it looks like, rather the function of the Holy Spirit in and through us. We could sit at the table and do devotions each morning and still have distracted hearts. We could play worship music all day and still be replaying bitterness in our minds over something someone did to us. We could demand that our children be kind, while neglecting the need for partnership with the Holy Spirit through prayer in the secret place. Often times as parents, we can get distracted by our child's behavior and put it first; we demand a proper form of attitude, behavior, speech, etiquette, and catechism, when all the while there is a function of the Spirit that is being hindered, untrained, and ignored.

Let's remember that the Jews rejected Jesus ultimately because they were expecting a king to come in grandeur; an Instagram-worthy story. Instead, they were presented with a mustard seed; a function of the kingdom that, for thousands of years, has produced the biggest and most abundant fruit this earth will ever see! I admonish us to not despise the small beginnings of the kingdom: the small corrections of the Spirit, the surrendering of the heart, the quiet moments in the secret places. Through cultivation, obedience, and partnership, THIS is what will produce much fruit in you, in your children and in your home all the days of your lives!

POSITION OF PRAYER

Jesus was the ultimate kingdom example of being positioned in prayer. He taught on prayer, went away to pray, and He encouraged His disciples to pray. Praying for your children is, without question, the most important service you will ever do for them. You can clothe them, feed them, bring them to church, educate them, and correct their behavior, but none of those things alone will truly develop them like seeking the Lord on their behalf. Notice how I said to seek the Lord on *their* behalf? I believe this is imperative to address because often times we are tempted to allow our prayers to settle over the mountains of *our* disapproval of their behavior or *our* hopes of their future. We might find ourselves crying out to God to help them obey us, respect us more, love others well, choose the right spouse, stop giving their attention to social media, or being careful not to have inappropriate affections for others. These prayers, although seemingly noble, are really a reflection of the fears we hold in our hearts. Since we've spent a previous section on love-based parenting vs.

fear-based parenting, I won't redundantly walk down that path of instruction, however I will build off the wisdom of its message—we are not assigned to change the fruit of our child's life by praying fearfully for their every move. Rather, we are called to walk intimately with Jesus and continue to advocate for the souls of our nations by partnering with the Holy Spirit concerning both their present and their future. Instead of praying that they would respect us more, pray that they would encounter Jesus deeper. Before praying that they would love others better, pray that they would love Jesus more and that God would empower them to know how deeply they are loved. More than praying that they would not give their attention and affection to social media or pornography, pray that they would be consumed with giving all attention and affection to Jesus! You are getting my point here, if your kids are walking closely with the Holy Spirit, loving God, and being loved by Him, consumed with affection for Jesus and obeying Him, then they will naturally respect you more, love better, obey authority, and have hope for their future. It does not mean they will never fall or fail, but your faith-based prayers will drive them to the throne so when they fail, they will bounce back quickly because Jesus is the center. Because our children are always watching us, don't forget that when you pray, they will know to pray, so promote faith-driven prayers in the home daily!

> "KEEP TRUSTING IN THE LORD AND DO WHAT IS RIGHT IN HIS EYES. FIX YOUR HEART ON THE PROMISES OF GOD, AND YOU WILL DWELL IN THE LAND, FEASTING ON HIS FAITHFULNESS. FIND YOUR DELIGHT AND TRUE PLEASURE IN YAHWEH, AND HE WILL GIVE YOU WHAT YOU DESIRE THE MOST. GIVE GOD THE RIGHT TO DIRECT YOUR LIFE, AND AS YOU TRUST HIM ALONG THE WAY, YOU WILL FIND HE PULLED IT OFF PERFECTLY." – **PSALM 37:3-5 (TPT)**

CHILDLIKE FAITH

> "LET THE LITTLE CHILDREN COME TO ME; DO NOT STOP THEM; FOR IT IS TO SUCH AS THESE THAT THE KINGDOM OF GOD BELONGS. TRULY I TELL YOU, WHOEVER DOES NOT RECEIVE THE KINGDOM OF GOD AS A LITTLE CHILD WILL NEVER ENTER IT." – **MARK 10:14-15**

This verse reveals a compelling truth; receiving the kingdom of God is the first step of promoting a kingdom culture in your home. Let's note here in Mark's passage that it's more than just receiving, Jesus says to receive the kingdom of God as a little child, or you will never enter it. How do children receive? Children receive gifts quite openly, unapologetically and with much excitement. They rarely stop to doubt if they deserve the gift or question the heart of the giver. Children tend to approach life with faith, wonder, awe, and adventure. They often run towards life with very little suspicion, worry, or burden. This is how we must receive and promote the kingdom of God; as little children would. As a very young mom, the Holy Spirit began to teach me through the lives of my nations how to receive the kingdom of God and His grace daily, and I often say now that I didn't just raise my children, they raised me. After two decades of walking with Jesus, there are seasons of my life when I am tempted to get cynical about the world, life, and even kingdom things. I constantly ask God to search my heart and find hardened places that I've allowed hurt and pain to jade my childlike function in receiving His kingdom, and when He highlights anything, I repent and receive grace for healing and fresh eyes to receive again. This can happen to all of us as we walk with the Lord - what once caused us to stand in awe now causes us to yawn and shrug our shoulders. I am convinced that the kingdom is alive in us in Christ, and we choose each day how we will receive Him. Will we give cheerfully in faith as we once did, or will we begin to complain that we don't like the way the church is spending our money? Will we forgive freely and compassionately out of gratefulness for what Jesus has rescued us from, or will we begin weighing another's sins and allow our hearts to become distant? As you allow God to keep your heart childlike, encourage your nations to keep the perspective of trust, simplicity, and wild faith even as they grow older, and never stop letting them teach you the awe and wonder of life!

GENEROSITY

> "GIVE, AND IT WILL BE GIVEN TO YOU. A GOOD MEASURE, PRESSED DOWN, SHAKEN TOGETHER, RUNNING OVER, WILL BE PUT INTO YOUR LAP. FOR WITH THE MEASURE YOU USE, IT WILL BE MEASURED BACK TO YOU." – **LUKE 6:38**

"Make as much as you can, for as long as you can, and give as much as you can away." This is a mantra that I have spoken regularly to my kids as they have grown and started working consistent jobs. Tithing is scriptural and we do teach it; however, generosity is emphasized more in the New Testament than tithing because tithing is typically tethered to just giving what is expected, whereas generosity is about reaching deeper into your heart and giving openly as much as the Lord will ask of you. Generosity is about giving away more than just money, it's giving time, talent, gifts, love, and service. Generosity is a valuable currency of the kingdom and reveals the heart of God towards His children. Jesus gave the best wine when no one would have cared (**John 2:10**), He multiplied more than enough bread and fish to the multitudes (**Matthew 14:20**), and though one drop of Jesus' precious blood would have been enough to satisfy Calvary, He bled more than enough, not by the cruelty of God, but by the generosity of Christ (**John 19:33-34**). When there are needs to be

filled and opportunities to give, we cultivate generosity in our home by asking each of our kids to pray and ask the Lord where He wants them to give and how much, this allows them to enter into a partnership with Him, not just obeying our commands to give simply because it's the right thing to do. Teaching our nations the discipline of giving and how to partner with what the Lord puts on their hearts for generosity produces lasting fruit in their lives.

CONFESSION AND FORGIVENESS

"Mom, I need to talk to you about something." Evelyn had that tone in her voice that I had heard from my children a time or two before; whether it was because of a broken vase, a stolen toy, a wounded sibling, or chocolate shake spilled on the carpet, it's that same sound; the sound of conviction leading to confession. The word confession feels like a "four-letter word" in the church today. We don't like to talk about the reality of sin let alone actually confessing them to others. Maybe it's because we've been beaten with legalism over the years, or because we mistake confession for shame and guilt, or because we are surrounded with a culture that compromises and makes sin feel too normal to call out as if it's really as bad as God says it is. Whatever the reason we don't like to talk about confession, I believe it is a primary reason that we do not occupy the position of freedom and live to the fullest the Spirit has to offer. Evelyn sat me on her bed and began to explain that she had been cheating on her math lessons for almost half the school year by logging into my parent portal and looking at the answers. She described how she had ignored the conviction of the Spirit, which turned into sitting in a vat of shame for months as this choice she'd made loomed over her. She explained that it was stealing her joy, giving her anxiety, and shame was causing her to be distant from me, so through teary eyes she proceeded to release it to me for healing. I have mentored and counseled many people

over the years, most who proclaim to be Christian, and one of the most frequent observations I've made is that shame consumes the heart like a plague without discrimination. Shame creates bondage and confusion, and keeps a person blinded to intimacy with God and others. Shame was introduced in the garden through hiding; when Adam and Eve sinned, they hid from God instead of confronting their actions in order to be healed. Shame pushed them away instead of drawing them close.

> "THEREFORE, CONFESS YOUR SINS TO ONE ANOTHER AND PRAY FOR ONE ANOTHER, THAT YOU MAY BE HEALED. THE PRAYER OF THE RIGHTEOUS PERSON HAS GREAT POWER AS IT IS WORKING."
> – JAMES 5:16

According to James, confession does two things for us: it brings us closer to each other in prayer, and it heals us. Confession is an act of exposing sin and drawing us to holiness, while hiding sin causes shame and pushes us further from the Holy One. Confession is something that I have personally practiced for years but it's an area that we haven't put emphasis on cultivating in our home until recently. We're still trying to figure out how to steer our ship in this direction, but I have felt the Lord inviting my family into the place of honest confession with one another SO THAT we can experience the fullness of healing and power in the Holy Ghost. I want to make it normal in my heart and my home to confront sin and be healed, instead of hiding it and being bound to shame cycles!

> "BEARING WITH ONE ANOTHER, AND FORGIVING EACH OTHER, WHOEVER HAS A COMPLAINT AGAINST ANYONE; JUST AS THE LORD FORGAVE YOU, SO MUST YOU DO ALSO." – COLOSSIANS 3:13

Just as confession brings closeness through vulnerability and prayer, forgiveness brings healing by us giving away what we first receive from God. If we don't see a need to be forgiven and brought into righteousness through Christ, how can we expect to see a need to extend that forgiveness to others? If then we don't see a need to confess and be healed through prayer, then how can we see a need to extend forgiveness to those who cross us? When we understand our own abilities to fall short, receiving the mercy of God, we can open our hearts to see others with the same compassion we are shown. Forgiving others is not a feeling, it's an act of obedience. Likewise, forgiveness is not a one and done action, it's a lifestyle lived day in and day out. Although Evelyn's actions of cheating on her math felt disrespectful to me, I chose to see her as God sees her and extend the forgiveness that I had first been given by Christ. The natural consequences of her choices were heavy enough since she had to redo the entire math curriculum over the summer instead of hanging out with friends.

There will be opportunities to forgive every single day of life because we live in a fallen world with humanity in process. We cultivate kingdom forgiveness in our homes by confessing our short comings to each other, receiving mercy and healing, and then extending forgiveness to others regularly as an act of surrender and obedience. When we continue this rhythm of confession and forgiveness, our homes will then be places of healing and holiness. Forgiveness is one of the most important elements of kingdom culture because it's the crown jewel of our salvation– we forgive because He first forgave us.

There are many more kingdom attributes to cultivate in the home, I could write an entire book just on these topics. Since it wouldn't be prudent to expound on everything, I'll drop a few more ideas below that you can explore on your own to promote in your home. Remember that kingdom culture starts with receiving it in yourself and is then cultivated in your home through intentionality, connection, and lifestyle.

TOPICS TO EXPLORE:

- **Discipline** – James 1:22, "BE DOERS OF THE WORD, AND NOT HEARERS ONLY, DECEIVING YOURSELVES." Discipleship is living out our salvation through discipline and lifestyle.

- **Discernment and Deliverance** – James 4:7, "SUBMIT THEREFORE TO GOD, BUT RESIST THE DEVIL AND HE WILL FLEE FROM YOU." Teaching spiritual discernment and spiritual warfare will prepare your children to live a life of freedom.

- **Love** – 1 Corinthians 13 explains God as love and the attributes of the God kind of love. There is a document titled "The God kind of Love" that we've had hanging in our home for years, and it beautifully articulates love from this scripture in 1 Corinthians. You're welcome to download it from our website under the toolbox tab for free: www.occupy-freedom.com

- **Honor** – Romans 12:10, "BE DEVOTED TO ONE ANOTHER IN LOVE. HONOR ONE ANOTHER ABOVE YOURSELVES." I will touch on this topic in more depth in the next chapter, but cultivating honor in your home is about promoting and calling out the gold in each other and reminding one another of who we are and Who we belong to!

PRAYER

Jesus, thank you that you are kingdom culture. Lord, I lean into you to show me how to receive the kingdom as a child. I want to know your heart and culture internally so that I can promote it in my home, my nations, and the world around me. Root me and ground me in your love, strengthen me in the inner man and build me up in You so that my home would become a safe haven of the Holy Spirit. I pray that when people walk into my home, they feel the power of your Spirit, that they would be healed, restored, and delivered instantly by your presence. I pray that when my children see me, they see you, and when they hear me, they hear you. Let my household reflect worship, honor, generosity, and love, and let it first start with me. Search my heart and find any way within me that is not of you and purify me to reflect who I am in you. I place my anchor in you, Jesus, Amen!

REFLECTION/DISCUSSION QUESTIONS:

1. What areas do I need to receive the kingdom afresh like a child? *(generosity, healing, deliverance, forgiveness, God's love, etc.)*

2. Are there areas that I have the form of kingdom in my home, but the function of the Spirit is hindered? *(i.e. we memorize scripture, but I don't have wisdom/revelation of the knowledge of God)*

3. What are some kingdom attributes that I feel the Holy Spirit inviting me to search more in the scriptures? *(i.e. Any topics that are listed above)*

CHAPTER 7

THE FUNNY THING IS...

*"Parenting without a sense of humor is like being an accountant who sucks at math." – **Amber Dusik***

L ife was heavy growing up; we dealt with an abundance of pain, disappointment, and dysfunction. Sometimes we lacked money, furniture, hot water, or groceries, but one thing we never lacked in our household was humor. I vividly remember my mom's witty jokes followed by her belly laugh that included a snort at the end. I can still see my dad's lighthearted playfulness as he talked with a funny voice or busted a funky dance move at the drop of a hat. Even though we didn't all live under the same roof, my parents simultaneously instilled in me the importance of joy and laughter in life, and it's been a treasure that I continue to draw on as I raise my nations.

Humor is something we don't often associate with successful parenting, and I was tempted to leave this short chapter out of the book for the sake of continuity. But I've come to find over the years that laughter is just as essential as the most disciplined life lesson I could ever teach my nations, and I felt the Lord wanted me to share it with you. The health benefits of laughter are staggering; laughing boosts our immunity, improves heart health, increases longevity, eases pain, lowers stress, changes our perspective, improves depression, and more. God's kindness has given you and your nations an anti-dote to the heaviness of the human experience as He "FILLS YOUR MOUTH WITH LAUGHTER AND YOUR LIPS WITH SHOUTS OF JOY" **- Job 8:21.**

IT'S JUST LIFE AFTER ALL

Laughter gives us the right perspective on life.

It was Christmas morning and all seven of us gathered in the living room, my scratch caramel rolls were in the oven, and I was sipping my coffee watching with anticipation as Maiya opened her gift from David. She ripped the paper off the box and care-fully opened the lid with a smile of excitement on her face. Ruf-fling through the tissue paper, her smile turned to a slightly puzzled and amused look as she lifted what appeared to be a used band-aid from the box. We all leaned forward asking in various ways, *"What is that?"* when David piped up, *"Oh THAT's where that went!"* The whole family burst into belly-laughter as David explained how he had lost his band-aid while he was wrapping gifts and never figured out what happened to it.

"Having children is a lot like living in a frat house:
nobody sleeps, everything is broken, and there's a lot
*of throwing up." – **Ray Romano***

Life feels a lot like an old T.V. sitcom sometimes. Maybe that's why my family loves reruns of the show "Everybody Loves Raymond" so much, it's just so relatable. As I type this, I can hear the witty one-liners and the opening piano to the show—it's like a tractor beam for our family; when the opening piano starts playing, everyone emerges from their rooms to sit in the living room and watch the show, share a snack, and connect. It's been such a consistent connector for us that Matthew has told me that when he moves out, he plans to come back often just to have coffee and watch Raymond for a sense of normalcy. Sitcoms tend to take the human experience and find the ridiculous humor in it all. I believe humor is a grace that God has given to help us connect to our humanity while bringing balance to the heavy emotions we experience daily. **Ecclesiastes 3:4** reminds us that there is, "A TIME TO WEEP AND A TIME TO LAUGH, A TIME TO MOURN AND A TIME TO DANCE." Raising our nations is a sobering assignment and it can become tempting to hunker down under the weight of the decisions we need to make, problems to solve, and messes to tackle, but God's mercy beckons us to be strengthened in His joy and embrace our human experience as worship unto Him. Whether I'm cleaning up body fluids, gluing lamps back together, or fishing a cocklebur out of my toddler's nostril (true story), God has had to remind me that while raising these nations is eternal business, the human experience is just life after all!

STITCHES & SPANK-A-THONS

Humor invites us to enjoy the mundane of life.

My kids used to play a game where Maiya would sit on the floor while the three younger ones ran laps around the basement, and she would try to spank them as they ran by, they called this game the spank-a-thon, and they laugh about the memory to this day. I think the spank-a-thon game accurately depicts how I felt at times in the mundane of raising my nations—just running laps while life tried to spank me. I remember times when I literally cried over spilled milk because I was so tired of doing the same thing over and over again; I would cry over the spilled milk, and then I would laugh at my crying about it. The ordinary tasks of life can seem meaningless, and laughter has a way of connecting us to the beauty of the process. I have come to find that it isn't the grandiose moments in life that capture God's attention the most. Rather, the mundane of creation is God's favorite part; He intricately designed the heart to beat 100,000 times per day and made the sun rise and set every single day without fail. He takes delight in watching us fold laundry, feed the cat, grocery shop, brush our teeth, and read books to our babies. Worship is finding joy in the everyday mundane details that God has given us to steward. Finding the humor in life helps change our view and invites us to thrive in the seemingly ordinary and repetitive tasks.

I don't know about you, but I get frustrated in seasons when it seems like I'm asking my children over and over again to do their chores, and I remember a time when humor invited me to enjoy the process. I had asked Matthew to feed Smoo, our family cat, and he forgot, so I asked him again. About an hour after I asked him the second time, the cat came to me and started meowing, which indicated she had not been fed, so she was snitching—or informing me. I asked, *"Matthew, did you feed the cat?!?"* His silence was enough to let me know he hadn't done his chore, so I gave him a short "talk". As he made his way to the storage room to get her food, Smoo ran to him and I heard him say to her under his breath, *"Snitches get stitches, Smoo!"* As I laughed at the interaction, it changed my perspective and reminded me that God has to be patient with my mundane process too, and, even through repetitive correction, He is always delighted to love me and cheer me on. Whether I am giving haircuts, folding laundry, or arguing with my nations because the cat isn't being fed on time, it's in the beautiful mundane process that we've learned to find the humor amid the spank-a-thon called life!

> "HELP US TO REMEMBER THAT OUR DAYS ARE NUMBERED AND HELP US TO INTERPRET OUR LIVES CORRECTLY." **PSALM 90:12 TPT**

THE MONA JILL

Laughter cultivates friendship and connection.

We have always loved to play games as a family. As our nations have grown over the seasons, the types of games we play have changed to suit their age levels and attention spans. Currently, the game we play most often is one called "Quiplash"—an online word game that requires cleverness and quick wit. There are many one-liners that we have created in this game that have become sources of ongoing laughter in our family time. Games can be a great way to cultivate laughter with your nations, and sharing those moments with them will form a common bond and friendship that lasts a lifetime. People often ask, *is it appropriate for a parent to be friends with their child?* Most psychology experts will initially say that it's not appropriate to consider yourself your child's "friend" because a parent's role is to set boundaries and maintain authority, and friendship tends to blur those lines. I wonder, though, can there be a healthy balance of friendship and authority? Let's look at the greatest example of relationship that we have—Jesus.

> "THIS IS MY COMMANDMENT, THAT YOU LOVE ONE ANOTHER AS I HAVE LOVED YOU. GREATER LOVE HAS NO ONE THAN THIS, THAT SOMEONE LAY DOWN HIS LIFE FOR HIS FRIENDS. YOU ARE MY FRIENDS IF YOU DO WHAT I COMMAND YOU. NO LONGER DO I CALL YOU SERVANTS, FOR THE SERVANT DOES NOT KNOW WHAT HIS MASTER IS DOING; BUT I HAVE CALLED YOU FRIENDS, FOR ALL THAT I HAVE HEARD FROM MY FATHER I HAVE MADE KNOWN TO YOU."
> **-JOHN 15:12-15**

Jesus calls us friends. A friend by definition is *one attached to another by affection or esteem; one that is of the same nation, party, or group.*[8] Jesus says that we are mutual friends, attached by affection, recognizing that we belong to the same nation. Scriptures also call Jesus Adonai—our Lord and Master: One that has authority over us. Could it be that God designed us to be in a healthy relationship with Him both as authority *and* friend? I believe Jesus sets a clear and healthy example of One who, as our authority, sets boundaries, yet is still mutually attached to us with affection. I agree that being in unhealthy friendships with our children can be a danger to their long-term development if we are trying to make up for our past hurts, manipulating them, or seeking to skirt responsibility. Our nations need us to lead them with discipline, boundaries, and strength, and I also see the beauty in calling them friends with fond affection... just as Jesus does for us. Don't be afraid to let laughter create a healthy connection and friendship with your nations, this is where trust and vulnerability are born.

DON'T GIVE ME THAT!

Laughter is an expression of faith through the storms of life.

When Matthew was three, he wanted to be an elephant for Halloween, so we found him a one-piece elephant costume with the hood that doubled as the elephant head. When he put the costume on, he realized that the elephant didn't have pants on and felt he would be embarrassed by the exposure. He decided the elephant costume would be more bearable if he put tighty whities over the top, so that's just what he did. We have videos of him riding his little Razor scooter in his elephant costume, wearing tighty whities over the top, while the neighbors looked on in amusement. Some things in life are just funny for no reason—underpants are one of them. Life can be like the proverbial elephant in the room, we can be faced with difficult situations and feel as if it's exposing our weakness. We might be tempted to cover the problem to make it more bearable for ourselves or others, but often the issues grow instead of going away. Laughter has a way of drawing out difficulty and giving us courage and faith to overcome.

There was a season of our life when our four nations were between the ages of two and twelve, and we had just been through several major life transitions, one of them being Justin's career. He had gone from having a stable, salaried position to full commission, gone for days at a time, traveling the state of Minnesota. We had no money—we were so broke we couldn't even pay attention, as my mom would say. Our bills were overdue, we shopped at the food shelf, and we entertained ourselves by putting on talent shows or watching Bob Ross while I taught the kids how to cross-stitch. Life was challenging and there were times that the stress of it all would break me. I remember the Lord was healing me from the spirit of anger during those years as well, anger was the elephant that had followed me since I was a little girl trying to make sense of my trauma and pain. I didn't want to pass this anger to the next generation, so I decided to accept the Lord's invitation to stop covering for it and start confronting it. There were some hard days and amid the season, my 5-year-old drew me a card with a sweet message inside: *"Your hugs are like marshmallows. Thanks for not blowing a gasket at me. I love that you're a great mom."* Those moments of honesty and laughter connected us through challenging times; laughter was our breakthrough from weeping to dancing. "WEEPING MAY LAST FOR THE NIGHT, BUT A SHOUT OF JOY COMES IN THE MORNING"**- Psalm 30:5.** Laughter was our defiant trust in God in the face of fear, "SHE IS CLOTHED WITH STRENGTH AND DIGNITY, AND SHE LAUGHS WITHOUT FEAR OF THE FUTURE"**- Proverbs 31:25**. We have faced many trials and hardships together as a family, and through it all, we laugh, because we know that God is good at what He does, and He always pulls it off perfectly!

"There's no such thing as a perfect parent. So just be a real one."
– Sue Atkins

CHICKEN-DI-POOP

Humor invites vulnerability.

I spent the whole day slow-cooking beef tips and gravy for dinner. I mashed the potatoes, set the table, and called my family to join me. David called out from his bedroom, *"Mom, what are we having? I want to know what to wear!"* I gave him a rundown of the menu and asked him to come quickly. As we sat down to pray, David came out of his bedroom and took his seat wearing a t-shirt on his head, a bathrobe tightly wrapped around his body, and a chip clip firmly placed on his nose. I broke into laughter as I received the message loud and clear—*I do not like what is being served for dinner tonight!* This was the same child that lovingly renamed my Chicken Divan, "chicken-di-poop", because he was not a big fan. This wasn't the first, nor would it be the last time David would protest my choices for dinner—among other things. Humor can extend an invitation for us to be vulnerable with one another. There are feelings in life that are hard to express; we want to share our thoughts, but it can be difficult to know how. When we laugh, we are letting others see into our hearts: what we like and don't like, our hopes, our dreams, our pain, and our fears. One of the health benefits of laughter is that it lessens anxiety and reverses depression, so when you laugh with your nations, you're helping to ease their stress and bring health to their hearts, which creates trust and connection with them.

GOTTA LOVE THE DANISH!

Laughter creates lifelong memories.

Halfway into his pastry, our four-year-old David blurted out, *"Gotta love the Danish!"* Where he learned that statement, I do not know, but what I do know is that our family has a language, a dialect that we speak with one another to remain connected and to communicate our hearts. It all started with scrapbooking. Our nations communicated at very early ages and any words they didn't know; they would just make up. Words like Crailmus (annoying), Grizzly (my foot fell asleep), and congenious (really smart) would make a frequent appearance in our conversations, so I decided to start writing down these funny memories for their scrapbooks. Little did I know those toddler phrases would turn into witty expressions and continue to evolve over the seasons. Whether we're giving one another a hard time, sharing Inside jokes, witty quips, one-liners, or mispronunciations adopted into our vocabulary, we've always had a way of knowing what each other means even when it doesn't make sense. Humor has created a safe space for vulnerability, faith, healthy hearts, and connections. There are times when the humor has to be reined in because the jokes start getting too sarcastic, but creating balance is always an important and ongoing discipline of life.

Laughter creates memories. Life is a series of moments and someday the moments will be memories. We choose the kind of memories we will have by how we respond to our moments. Whatever season you find yourself in, ask yourself, *"What kind of memory do I want this moment to be?"* Then respond accordingly. My prayer for you is not necessarily that this journey of parenting would be a perfect experience, but that there would be opportunities for you to respond well to each moment you're given, so that raising your nations will be impactful, life-changing, and joy-filled!

PRAYER

God, thank you for the gift of humor! Thank you that laughter is your mercy gift to us to balance the human experience, and it brings life to our bodies and health to our hearts. Help me to embrace your design for laughter in my life and the lives of my nations, so we can be healthy, joy-filled, and full of your Spirit. I realize that the mundane of this life can be overwhelming, but I want to live every part of it as worship unto you, Lord. Give me a fresh perspective of my days and set me free to dance, laugh, love, and enjoy raising my nations. In Your precious name, Amen!

REFLECTION/DISCUSSION QUESTIONS:

1. How has laughter brought you through the storms of life?

2. How do you want God to help you grow in joy and laughter?

3. What are some things that your family does together that brings joy and laughter?

CHAPTER 8

INVESTING IN THE TWEENS, TEENS, AND BEYOND

"There are two lasting bequests we can give to our children. One is roots. The other is wings." **Hodding Carter Jr.**

One of the blessings I've enjoyed on our homeschooling journey is the flexibility to live life with my kids at very culturally abnormal times of day. Grocery shopping at 10am while everyone is at work, playing at the park after lunch when most of the kids are in school, or going to Sea Life at the Mall of America on a weekday when it's quiet. On a particular Wednesday, my daughter, Evelyn, and I decided to go to Panera and grab some lunch in between classes that day. As we were chatting over some chicken wild rice soup and mac and cheese, I asked her what she felt was the most challenging thing she's noticed about being a teenager. She said, *"It's challenging when you feel like some adults don't respect you or have confidence in you because of your age and process. We are capable of much more than adults give us credit for."* As I ate my soup and listened to her share her heart with me, I felt the sobering burden of the next generation who has and is always crying out for the same thing, grace to process with the confidence to contribute.

The teen years can be hard, how can we have good relationships with our teenage nations? As I've considered this question thoughtfully, I've determined the primary thing that makes teenagers so challenging in our adult minds is that we forget how we felt when we were once in the same process they are. We lose memory of the stupid decisions we've made, the tension we faced, and the heaviness we endured; therefore, we lose our humility in remembering what God has brought us through. Tweens and teens ARE challenging, Lord, don't we know it! It takes an incredible amount of grace to be in a healthy relationship with a growing teenager, because they are in an intense process of life. Their brains aren't fully developed, yet they're dealing with heavy hormones and looming emotions, all the while feeling this deep sense that they somehow need to start owning their life with no idea how to do it. Yes, tweens and teens take a lot of grace, but so do toddlers, so do adults, so do you, and so do I. Every person on earth takes a certain amount of grace to be in relationship with, teenagers just require a bit more for a season.

WHAT WERE YOU THINKING?!

It was a sunny summer day; I was in my garden when I heard a *POP! CRACK!* And then a moment of silence followed by my husband saying, *"what were you thinking?!"* As I approached the scene, my eye caught the sight of a shattered glass backboard on the basketball hoop, a bb gun in the hands of my young teenage son, and astonishment on his face. He had been tracking a bird when it flew behind the clear backboard and without considering that there was glass between the bird and his pellets, he fired away!

Have you ever wondered what in tarnation your kid was thinking when they did something that seemed to lack…thorough consideration? I have and I know my parents have said it to me too! Countless times when my kids have done something dicey, I have either thought or said out loud, *"What in salvation were you thinking?!"* Their answer is usually along the lines of, *"Uh, I don't know".* The fact is they really don't know, they aren't thinking, they are primarily feeling and doing. The thinking part comes later when they realize at the exact same moment you do just how foolish their actions were, and funny enough, they're just as perplexed as you are!

According to the University of Rochester Health Encyclopedia, "The rational part of a teen's brain isn't fully developed and won't be until age 25 or so. In fact, recent research has found that adult and teen brains work differently. Adults think with the prefrontal cortex, the brain's rational part. This is the part of the brain that responds to situations with good judgment and an awareness of long-term consequences. Teens process information with the amygdala. This is the emotional part. In teen's brains, the connections between the emotional part of the brain and the decision-making center are still developing— and not necessarily at the same rate. That's why when teens experience overwhelming emotional input, they can't explain later what they were thinking. They weren't thinking as much as they were feeling."[9]

In a nutshell, your children's bodies are growing faster than their sense of direction; although they will begin to look like an adult, they could very well lack the basic reasoning of an adult, don't forget you were that age once upon a time! When you pursue your nations, especially young teens, try to let go of your need to understand the logic behind what they feel and do, because it doesn't exist, and you will only exhaust yourself coming at it from that angle. Instead of resisting their emotional tendencies, get to know their style of processing those emotions so that you can come along side of them and guide them through it. That's the beauty of being a parent (and grandparent), you get to use your experiences, victories, and failures to guide and influence the heart and mind of your kids and then your grandkids. You don't have to understand them completely, you just need to know the One who does and extend grace as needed.

THE INFLUENCE OF RELATIONSHIP

I walked into our supply room on a Wednesday morning with my coffee in hand and flipped on the light switch to take a look at my desk calendar, making sure I knew all that my family had going on for the rest of the week. I happen to be a tactile person, so I like to use a pencil to write in my appointments, meetings, birthdays, and events on a large paper calendar. Said calendar then lays out in the open so I can walk past and look at it five times a day, so I don't forget anything. Maybe it's because I'm forgetful, or simple, or complicated, or just old fashioned, but it's seriously the only way my brain retains the whirlwind of events our family has going on. As I stood there staring down to the week sipping my coffee, I saw a few extra words on the calendar for Tuesday, Wednesday, and Thursday. In egg-shaped, pre-teen boy handwriting were the words, *"Bad day"*, *"Bad day"*, and *"Going to be another bad day"*.

You see, our younger son, David, has always been a bit more "Ecclesiastical" in his life processes. He is our kid who will get frustrated with the mundane, the regular, and the repetitive, seeking out variety in everything. The depravity of the world tends to weigh a little heavier on his heart and eat a little deeper at his soul. He can be moody, stubborn, and a half-glass-empty kind of guy, who thinks that if you don't agree with him, then it must be because you just don't understand how he's explaining it. Simultaneously this precious boy of mine is the most attentive, loving, heart-felt, compassionate, and spiritually sensitive kid I know. He is always the first to express his undying love and affection for me at all hours of the day and cannot stand when someone he loves is hurting in any way. If you cry, he cries. If you laugh, he laughs. If you're downtrodden, he's always attentive to be a listening ear. If he says, *"I hate you"* under his pre-teen, hormone-infused breath when no one can hear, he is the kid who will come clean with tears streaming down his face at bedtime because he just cannot bear to have that evil against you in his heart. He will well up with tears when we're praying as he senses the Holy Spirit, and as a matter of fact, the week that he had expressed his complaints on our family calendar was the same week he sat on the couch next to me sharing his heart for the lost and how he was feeling a pull to pray more, wanting to capture what God was saying to him. As a mom, when I look at his crummy attitude etched in no.2 pencil lead on a random Tuesday, I am tempted to simply rebuke him and move on, but as a steward of his soul I've learned to see beyond the flesh and guide him to press into the prophetic pull that is happening in his spirit. When you deal with the mere surface of your teenager's life, you can adjust their behavior, but when you take the time to reach in deeper to their heart, your relationship with them will influence their soul.

Being relationship-focused with your tweens and teens means you are looking deeper into each circumstance that presents itself in your relationship with them. You are looking for opportunities to cultivate connection and trust through lending yourself selflessly to their process. You may need to stop what you're doing at any given moment and sit with them, listen to them, play a game with them, or just be available for them. When your nations are little, you are often focused on safety, control, and stability, but as they begin to learn the responsibility of ownership, they need to know that you trust them to apply what you've taught them. They need to know that you are for *them*, not just what *you ideally want* for them. We show our teens that we are for them, by investing in deep, respectful relationship.

Relationship means you shift from telling them what is true to asking them what they want to know. Relationship is asking more questions and making less statements, which means you may have to forego the need to be right in order that they may respect you. Let's be honest, trying to win an argument with a teenager is much like catching a fish with your bare hands; next to impossible!

> *"When your nations are little, you are often focused on safety, control, and stability, but as they begin to learn the responsibility of ownership, they need to know that you trust them to apply what you've taught them."*

Keeping a relationship focus also means being interested in what they love or what they're doing even if it doesn't really appeal to you, because what you are really expressing is an interest in their unique heart and mind. As they grow you will find that they don't voluntarily come to you as much as they did when they were little and needy, you'll find yourself needing to pursue them and speak their love language. Ask them good questions and give them space to answer, no matter how long of a conversation it may be. You may have to stay up that extra 30 minutes when you're so tired you just want to go to sleep, and they want to discuss something important. When you are relationship-focused, you may sometimes need to put aside what you want to do to be involved with what they want; take the time to go watch their sports games and activities, cheering them on from the sidelines. I encourage you to grow with your kids, meet their friends and get to know who they're hanging out with, furthermore, get to know the parents of who they're hanging out with. If you find it challenging to meet the growing relational needs of your children, there are a treasure of options to help you:

- Read some great books on relationships and parenting.
- Pull wisdom from somebody you know, who has had success in this area.
- Find a Mentor.
- Most importantly, pray and ask God to show you creative ways to learn, grow, and become successful in relationships with your kids, He knows what they need!

The Holy Spirit knows and loves our children more than we ever could—even on our best days—so seek Him and let Him show you how to have a meaningful relationship with your kids. Personally, I had to do a lot of praying, reading, and seeking wisdom from others, because relationship-focused parenting wasn't a natural thing for me. Deep relationship and influence are certainly some things I've always wanted with my kids, because I understand how important it is for our whole family. It wasn't nurtured in me or modeled for me though, so I pray often along the way that God will continue to show me how to unlock the relational part of my heart and my mind. I pray daily that He would teach me how to know what my nations need, how to put down the things that I'm doing even when it's hard so that I can engage with them. I ask Him to lead me in putting aside my frustrations or my preferred communication styles in order to hear what my nations are saying, to learn how to listen more than I speak, how to love more than I judge, and how to think before I respond. When you find areas of relationship with your kids that are harder for you, don't take it as a defeat or failure, instead, let your weakness lead you to God's grace-strength. The weak areas are where your children are going to help you grow; you may think you're just raising your kids, but don't forget that God sent them to you to help you learn and grow as well—so embrace the journey!

Raising a teenager is hard, but being a teenager
is hard too, which is why our kids need someone
they trust to lean on, to come to for advice
and share their lives—the good, the bad and
the ugly. Having a front row seat in our kids' lives
is a far better place to be than sitting on
the highest bleacher. — **Raising Teens Today**

JESUS PLUS NOTHING

Have you ever asked your middle school or high school aged child
where they would spend eternity if they died today? Their answer
may shock you, and it may also give you the greatest insight into
their process you need in order to love them well. Trusting in Jesus
is the ultimate goal in raising nations, there is no higher motivation
to bring up our children than for them to love and be loved by their
Creator and Savior. However, I have found through research and
personal experience, that one of the greatest misconceptions that
teenagers grow up with is what I call a striving salvation: If I can be
a good person, I will be loved by God. When they realize that they
are imperfect, they begin to feel that their humanity has no place in
the love of God, thus they have two options to choose from: live in
shame via religious obligation or walk away altogether.

   I currently teach a Kingdom Worldview class to a group of 20-30
students ranging from 9th - 12th grade, and it has been an amazing and eye-opening experience to say the least. We dive into topics relating to origins, the existence of God, morality, what happens
after death, and how to engage culture. We'll explore some of these
topics in the next section of this book. Since the students I teach
primarily come from Christian families, most of them have at least
a foundation of the Christian faith—what Christians believe and
who Jesus is—however, they all come from different backgrounds,

denominations, and life dynamics, which makes for rich classroom discussion on most topics. One particular week in the first year I taught this class, we were diving into the concept of heaven and how we know there is an eternal extension to life after this life. I decided to explore salvation with the students, so I opened our class time together with the question, *"if you were to die today, where would you spend eternity?"* Expecting to get the typical Sunday school answers, I sat back on my heels ready for the discussion to be short. Instead, I was surprised with the answers I was given such as,

> *"I'm not sure, I haven't read my Bible in a while."*
>
> *"I think I would go to heaven, but I'm not sure because I don't live my life very good."*
>
> *"Probably heaven, but I don't feel very close to God right now."*

and many other variations of this answer that included words like probably, maybe, and I hope so. Pressing them a bit more I discovered that a large percentage of these young people related their personal behavior to their identity, their value, and the probability of God loving them. I had assumed that since they were brought up in church and knew basic Christian doctrine that they understood God's love for them on a relational grace level, but I was mistaken.

Leaving class that day, I felt like I had a two-ton block on my shoulders. More than any content I could possibly teach these students in this class, I wanted them to know how much God loved them regardless of what they've done or what they're going through. I wanted them to know that there is no amount of good works that will save them. I wanted them to feel the freedom of acknowledging their need for the Savior and rest in the finished work only He can provide. I prayed. And prayed. And prayed. *"Lord show me how to reach them."* The burden of the answers to this very simple yet eternally important truth was evident—many teenagers feel pressured to own a faith that they neither understand nor are prepared for.

As parents we often tend to emphasize scripture memorization, mealtime prayers, and morality, because we want to raise functional adults who bear fruit in their life to reflect Jesus. While this is a noble motive, we think we can achieve this by focusing on the fruit instead of the root. What I have noticed with the method of focusing on the fruit is that the message most often received by our teenagers is: *"the fruit of my life is what makes me worthy of love from God and people, so I better strive to be a better person."* Instead, the pure message of the gospel is that the love of God is what makes us worthy and the fruit in our lives will bear evidence that we understand we are loved and known by Him. I went back to my class the next week and hauled in a potted vegetable plant that had been sitting on my back patio, to use for an illustration. I plopped it down on the table and said, *"who can tell me what kind of plant this is?"*

"It's a pepper plant" yelled someone from the back.

"Yes, how did you know that?" I asked.

Silence... (Teenagers seem to hate to answer obvious questions) Finally, the silence broke, *"uh, because there are peppers growing on it?"*

I said, *"Good point, so you know what kind of plant it is or what seed DNA it bears because of the fruit on it, correct?"*

A resounding *"yea"* hit the room.

"Okay" I said, *"How did this fruit grow on the pepper plant? Did I craft it myself? Did I will it to be? Did the plant try really hard?"*

One student piped up, *"No, the peppers grow because it's just what the plant is created to do when the roots get water, nutrients and sunlight."*

I let her statement linger in the air for a few seconds so that everyone could ponder it. *"Interesting"* I announced, *"So, the peppers growing on this plant aren't what qualifies it to be a pepper plant, the peppers are the evidence that it is planted in a healthy place and receiving the proper nutrition to develop."*

You could have heard a pin drop in that room. Eyes were wide, hearts were engaged, and I could sense the Holy Spirit giving hope and courage to these young people. In this illustration I began to unravel the false perception that behavior was the doorway to love, and I helped knit together the truth that even though they will fail, they are loved, known, and valued by their Creator. The weeks following, I helped them unpack their identity in Christ and saw them come to life in such beautiful ways. It's such a sacred thing for us as parents to be able to look into the eyes of our nations and remind them repeatedly that they are not what they do, they are not what they have, and they are not what other people say or think about them. This message is the same message that God whispers to our hearts even as adults, how much more necessary is it for us to speak it often into these young people who are going through an intense process. Jesus plus NOTHING is the gospel; He is more than enough for you, for me, and for the nations we're raising!

THE ART OF LETTING GO

I lay in bed on a tear-soaked pillow, images of my four children when they were just babies and toddlers swam around my head. I sobbed and sobbed. Nobody could prepare me for the deep aching of my heart as I entered the years of letting go. I couldn't quite put my finger on why my heart was so heavy, I instinctively wanted to interpret it as sadness and pain, did I miss their littleness? Did I feel parent-shame for something? Was it fear of what my life was going to look like as they are nearing time to fly the nest? Maybe it was a little of each of these, but as I dialogued with the Lord about what was going on in my heart, I heard Him whisper, *"gratefulness."* That's it! Gratefulness, my heart was aching, longing, and bursting with gratefulness as I reflected on the years of holding babies, training littles, the years of teaching middle schoolers, guiding highschoolers and now the years of launching these young adults.

I opened my mouth and began to praise the Lord and express how grateful I was for His gift to me of these nations. I thanked Him for always leading me and guiding me as a mama. I praised Him for making a way for me to be home, homeschool, learn alongside them, and see them through each step of the way. I thanked Him for redeeming so many parts of my heart through raising them. I expressed gratitude for the ups and downs that have led to such rich relationships with each one of my children and I sat in awe of how miraculous this journey had really been. As I articulated each detail I was grateful for, the release of letting go became more easy, joyful, and sure.

Allowing God to help me navigate the tears and gratefulness, aligned my heart with His and I was suddenly quickened with excitement! I've spent all these years stewarding, shaping, praying, guiding, and imparting kingdom perspective to these beautiful humans and now I get to see the BEST part, the launching! Gratefulness flooded over me once again as I realized my relationship with them was not ending but beginning again in a deeper season. I have a front row view to their destiny.

I have such intimate and unique relationships with each one of my teenagers and young adults; not always easy, not always feel-good, and certainly not perfect, but we're connected, and we trust each other. A question that I get asked often is, *"How do you keep good relationships with your teens and young adult children?"* The first time someone with little ones asked me this question, I was caught off guard because I hadn't stopped to put a lot of thought into "how" I had good relationships with my kids. My eyes have been intentionally fixed on "Who" knows best for me and for my nations: Jesus. He has led me every step of the way. I ask the Holy Spirit at every turn what to do, how to respond, how to engage, and how to repent and grow. Through the process of allowing Him to transform my heart as a woman and a mother, I've grown the fruit of closeness to the people He's given me to steward in life. These are a few of the many things that the Lord has taught me in stewarding a relationship with my teenagers as I learn the art of letting go:

Pray first, respond if necessary. Teenagers have a lot to say, and they are constantly processing questions, discouragements, decisions, and longings. With their verbal process will come things that they say but don't really mean. Often as parents we want to jump on every word spoken, deed done, or attitude given, but I have found much wisdom in praying before I respond to the sharp arrows that are launched. A simple prayer that has carried me through near death explosions when I'm about ta SNAP! is, *"Lord, help me respond in love."* This prayer has centered my heart a million times when I feel like I don't know what's going on with my teens, and I feel them pushing me away or being ugly. Responding in love doesn't mean we condone or ignore their behavior; it means we respond with wisdom and compassion for their process instead of being more concerned about how it's making us feel.

Choose influence over control. When our children were little, we decided what was best for them: foods they ate, time they went to bed, friends they hung out with, and activities they were a part of. As our kids grew into pre-teens, I felt a nagging tension with these areas. I remember when Maiya was around twelve years old, we were all hanging out in the living room, and at some point, she got up and went into the refrigerator to grab a snack. Up to this point we regulated the eating situation with our littles, but she was five years older than her next sibling, and her independence came upon us so suddenly that her dad and I didn't know how to respond. We looked at each other and then shrugged our shoulders as we quickly realized she was indeed old enough to decide if she needed something to eat. It seems so oddly insignificant, but since Maiya was our first child to go through this transition, it perplexed

us! This pattern continued to create tension with each of our growing teens; every time they wanted to eat pizza at 10pm or let their
laundry pile up until they had no clothes to wear, my skin would
crawl, and we would argue. Each time, the Lord would remind me
that I had to shift from control to influence; from telling them what
was best, to trusting them to figure out what was best, even if they
learned the hard way. These teen nations want to make decisions
for themselves, and they want to know that we trust them to do
it. Influence is captured in your relationship with your teens when
they know that you are for them, not just for what you want for
them. They are going to fail, but they need to know that you trust
them to figure it out with the Lord, and when they know that you
trust them, they will grant you influence in their life, and they will
lean on your input more.

Ask more questions and make less statements. Remember,
teenagers are in an intense process emotionally, relationally, spiritually, and physically. They need guidance, but they have this overwhelming realization that they must figure out how to own their
ideas and decisions. The goal of raising nations is to bring them to
this place of ownership: owning their faith, their process, their relationships, their body care, and their choices. Asking them thought-
provoking questions is a great way to lead them to the water so they
can decide how to drink. When you give statements, you're sending
the message that you know best, and they must fall in line. When
you resist the urge to express your opinion about everything and
instead ask them good questions, the message you're sending with
it is that you trust them to figure out the best way forward based on
what you've sown into them already. I know you might be thinking,
"but my way is the best way", and that may be so, but it's your way,
not theirs. God has a unique journey for each one of us, and we
must give our teens a push to pursue Him, because He IS the way!
You can hold your ground, and argue so you can be right, or you

can choose to listen to their hearts and gain their respect, but you rarely can have both. Do you want to be right, or do you want to be respected?

Fiercely pursue them. As I mentioned earlier, our kids spend their younger years coloring our world and adventuring where we take them, and it makes relationship with them convenient. As they grow into their own, it becomes more inconvenient for us to connect with them so, it's important for us to intentionally pursue them on their unique journey. Teens often act like they don't need you, and it's probable that they don't even know that they need you, but instead of being offended, I want to encourage you to push past the inconveniences and take them on dates, get to know what they love and why, try new things with them, edify their likes and dislikes. Don't let the gap grow between you and your teenager just because you have to find a new way to relate to them. Pursuing them lets them know that you're interested in them, no matter how many things you may or may not have in common. Invest in your nations' seasons, pursue their heart, and mind, and let them teach you a new way to see the world!

INVESTING IN YOUR ADULT NATIONS

"I don't know who's being stretched more right now, her or you!" I was dialoguing with the Holy Spirit while putting in another load of laundry that day; the day after our second daughter, Evelyn, had left for YWAM and was settling into her new life in Kona, Hawaii. She had called earlier to explain some unexpected challenges that she faced upon arrival. My first instinct was to make some rescue phone calls and find a solution to her problem so that she would be comfortable. My mind was flipping through all the possible solutions and how I could make things better when I heard the Lord say, *"pray for her to lean into Me, not you this time."* It quickened me to remember that

Evelyn was an adult, and my goal was not for her to depend on me, it was for her to learn to independently depend on Jesus. So, I began to pray, not that her circumstances would just go away, but that she would pray and ask God to give her wisdom on what to do next and empower her to be stretched into new things. That's when the Holy Spirit made the opening statement of this section, *"I don't know who's being stretched more right now, her or you!"* I laughed and retorted, *"Oh, it's definitely ME that's being stretched here!"* Over the folding of my family's laundry, it became apparent that the following six months of Evelyn's adventures across the oceans and mission fields were going to stretch me and teach me a new level of trust: trusting God, trusting Evelyn, and trusting myself.

As I write this part of the book, Justin and I have two adult children: Maiya (25) and Evelyn (20) with Matthew rounding the corner to age eighteen this year and David going on sixteen. The investment in our adult nations' lives has been a bit of a learning curve that we are still new to, and I'm not sure I could have articulated my thoughts on it... until I experienced being in the delivery room while Maiya gave birth to her first child in December of 2023. Maiya asked Evelyn and I to be by her and her husband's side while she brought a daughter of their own into this world, one of the most sacred human experiences one could have. I was humbled and honored at the thought of being in the room for this moment in my daughter's life, but I must be honest, I was not prepared for how it would impact me in the most joyful and vulnerable of ways; the highs were really high, and the lows were really scary. To be by your adult child's side while they experience the intensity of living and giving life is wild and it comes with a great reminder that you'll never be done being your child's mom or dad. As our daughter has become such an incredible mama for herself, she has nestled back under my arm in a different way. Life is puzzling sometimes; we work so intricately to knit ourselves to our children, only to painstakingly loosen our grip on their lives as they grow up, recognizing that they need to become independently dependent on God. Then they return to our wing for support once again as they begin navigating the circle of life for themselves.

It was just two weeks after the birth of our granddaughter that we dropped Evelyn off at the airport to embark on her six-month journey with YWAM, and, as I mentioned previously, it has been a season that certainly stretched me more than I thought possible. As your nations become adults, they must transition into becoming independently dependent upon Jesus for their needs, but it doesn't mean you're done investing in them as their parent, it just means they need you to show up and invest in them in different ways.

CAN I GET A CONNECTION?

Growing up it was impressed upon my brother and I that when we turned eighteen our parents were "done." I guess that meant that they were on to the next thing for themselves and what ensued in our adult lives was up to us to figure out...good luck! Because I was pregnant at seventeen, I moved out and had my own place before I even graduated high school. I worked full time, finished my credits, and healed from a c-section while raising my daughter, all before I was even eighteen years old. I desired connection, help, and support, but was convinced that I had to do it all on my own and figure it out because my parents were, you know, done. Because I was raised to be independent in such a way, I was a very determined, capable, and driven person as I entered adulthood, but the negative side effect to it was that I didn't naturally have a need for closeness with my parents. What God would later show me is that DNA doesn't keep a family close, connection does. As a mother, I spent a substantial amount of time building connection with my four nations as they were little and growing, so I became afraid as they approached adulthood assuming it was normal for them to just move out and lose closeness with me. I wondered if there was a way to keep a connection with them through adulthood while encouraging and equipping them to be independently dependent on Jesus.

God created humans with a need for connection. In fact, most all living things survive and thrive on connection. If I gaze upon the most beautiful roses or taste the most delicious grapes, it's because they grow and fruit from connection to the main source of the plant, and cross pollinate with their surrounding community.

> "I AM THE VINE; YOU ARE THE BRANCHES. IF YOU REMAIN IN ME AND I IN YOU, YOU WILL BEAR MUCH FRUIT; APART FROM ME, YOU CAN DO NOTHING." – **JOHN 15:5**

My deepest core relationship is with God: Father, Son, and Holy Spirit. I do not pursue Christ out of obligation or convenience. I am passionate about the Lord; I want to live in His presence and know Him deeper every day because of connection. When I encounter Him in my failures or my victories, in my strengths or my weaknesses, and when He comforts me in the valleys and celebrates with me on the mountain tops, that connection makes me want more of Him. That connection is why I pursue Him. Religion demands pursuit out of obligation, not connection, and as Christ warned, religion is a thief of connection (**John 10**).

If I take this most important core relationship pattern with God and then apply it to the people in my natural life, it's the same scenario; I don't pursue relationships out of convenience or obligation, but out of connection. I want to be with people that I feel peaceful with, that I trust, that want to know me, and that I want to know. If I pursue a relationship and the connection feels futile or I feel shame, judgement, or isolation, then why would I want to be close? Intimacy essentially means In-to-me-see, which requires connection. When we think of raising our nations, it's not just a job for their younger years, we are investing our hearts into creating connection with them that will hopefully last a lifetime. What does it mean to create connection with our nations? Or anyone for that matter?

- **Connection is being willing to be vulnerable, transparent, and trustworthy.** When I'm hurting, need prayer or I am processing difficult decisions, I choose to invite my children into the process instead of hiding from them. This always comes with wisdom because not all things are appropriate for your children to understand or be involved with. Even so, invite your kids to pray and believe with you for healing, or share with them that you've been hurt and you're practicing forgiveness – without giving inappropriate details. Vulnerability teaches them that you are, in fact, human, and they can trust you as they become adults and have their own humanity to work through.

- **Connection is celebrating, honoring, and calling out the best in one another.** Listen, I tend to be a bit of a reformer at heart, and I can walk into a room and usually identify what needs to be improved within a short period of time. I do understand that God wants to use it as a gift, but, if I'm not careful, this perspective has and can easily become critical and nitpicky. There are times when I come home and, before I even say "hello" to my kids, I start pointing out all of what didn't get done instead of acknowledging their presence and honoring what did get done while I was gone. If you've been in any sort of relationship for any length of time, you'll understand that others' weaknesses can be glaringly easy to point out, that's why we do it so often. It takes an intentional heart to look past all of your nation's mistakes so you can encourage and honor their gifts and strengths. Sometimes this has to be practiced in order to feel natural, so in our household we practice what is called "honor time". Whether it's for someone's birthday, graduation, holidays, or just family time, we sit together and choose a person to honor, edify, encourage, prophesy, and speak life into. It's been a successful way to practice knowing one another by the spirit instead of the flesh, as the Apostle Paul put it (**2 Corinthians 5**).

- **Connection is asking more questions and making less statements.** You may be tired of me banging on this drum, but I will bang on it again because it's a vital part of raising strong nations. Have you ever been in a conversation with someone who asked really good questions that made you feel valuable and seen? I thank God that I have a couple of very dear friends that are so good at the art of making you feel like you're the only person in the room! On the contrary, have you ever found yourself in a conversation with a person that talked about themselves the whole time and you walked away feeling totally drained and unseen? I'm sure we've all been on the receiving AND the giving end of this scenario a time or two. We all have a natural desire for people to see us and to share what's going on in our life, our thoughts, our successes, our newest updates, but connection isn't created in the statements, it's created in the questions. When you ask good questions of your nations, you're letting them know that they're important, their process holds value, and that they have something important to give away and you're there for it! Good questions aren't just preference-based, *"how's it going?"*, *"Do you eat organic?"* Good questions pull out the treasure of the soul, *"how are you processing being a new parent?"*, *"What's been easy for you this week?"*, *"What's been a challenge?"*, or *"What's God been showing you lately?"* This is probably a good place for a reminder that connection is an intentional investment, not a convenience. Being interested in your nation's life as they grow into teens and young adults, even in the areas that you don't agree with or share a passion for, takes a surplus of intentionality.

One of the goals of parenting is to train our children to become independently dependent on Jesus for life, so that they can fulfill their purpose on the earth with Him. The hard part is becoming successful at this and realizing that our children will not always need us in the way they once did. They will all grow up and blossom in their uniqueness and our shared DNA alone will not guarantee closeness, but I am thoroughly convinced that we can stay close with our nations through adulthood if we take time to create and foster intentional connection with one another.

SOMEDAY

Someday the lawn will be mowed in straight lines. Someday There won't be pizza boxes hanging from the garage ceiling for knife throwing practice, and my chocolate stash won't be raided and left in crumbs when I have a craving. Someday my flat iron won't be missing at an essential moment of getting ready to fly out the door. Someday the wet towels won't decorate the bathroom floor, and the shower drain won't be clogged with hair. Someday there will be more than a teaspoon of creamer left in the fridge for my morning coffee. Someday there won't be heated arguments about who's better at bulking for basketball, who is taller, who can bench press more weight, or who used the last of the chocolate syrup. Someday I won't be yelling up the stairs before church like a crazy woman, issuing threats like, *"If butts are not in seats in the next two minutes....!"*

Someday I will be looking fondly on the beauty of the chaos that once lingered in our home. I will be thanking God for allowing me to be in the midst of it all while I sip my properly creamered coffee. Someday I will remember when I prayed for the grace to soak it in because I knew that someday all would be quiet and in order… and I would wish for the chaos to visit me once in a while. It is true what they say, "the days are long, but the years are short." I encourage you to keep margins; be intentional and soak up the highs and lows of the seasons, because you will take these memories with you and revisit them often with gratitude and joyfulness in your heart… someday.

PRAYER

God, I appreciate the unique journey that we all have to take through our teenage years. I recognize that I don't have all the answers to the challenges that my teen nations face or will face someday. I pray that you would give me a meek heart that I might learn from them just as much as I want them to learn from me! Teach me how to be a safe space for my teens to process life, their doubts, fears, temptations, and faith. Empower me to connect with them through intentionality and throw off apathy and convenience. My greatest prayer for my teens and young adults is that they know YOU, Jesus, that they would love YOU and serve YOU all the days of their life. I trust you with their outcome, thank you for doing what only You can do in Jesus' name, AMEN!

REFLECTION/DISCUSSION QUESTIONS:

1. If you have teenagers, what are some specific areas that you feel you are successful and areas that you need God to give you wisdom and help?

2. If you do not yet have teenagers, what do you want your relationship with your teens to look like and how is God inviting you to grow to fulfill that vision? (Example: a good listener, tender-hearted, generous, etc.)

3. The main question burning inside the heart of most teens is, "Are you for *me* or are you for what *you want* for me?" Ask the Holy Spirit to show you areas that you need to make this adjustment.

PART 2

Imparting a Kingdom
Worldview

"Keeping the big picture in mind is one of the most important things parents can do, and also one of the hardest"
– T. Berry Brazelton

Statistically it is said that the most predominant age kids will question their faith and turn away from God (if they're going to do so) will be the middle and high school years (6th-12th grade). Many young people have come forward and confided that they left their faith because they discovered that the church, their youth group leaders, or their parents could not sufficiently engage in discussion or answer their questions about God. It is possible that if we cannot engage with these questions, it may be because we as parents have not yet wrestled with our own intimate reality of what we believe and why. Therefore, I encourage you to allow this section to first permeate your own heart in any areas that yet need discovery before you guide your nations through. Keep in mind that you do not create a worldview for your children, you cultivate and shape a worldview that first lives in you; invest in your faith and then teach them how to invest in theirs.

This section of the book is intended to help launch good conversations surrounding foundational questions that our nations must ask as they come of age. At the end of each section or chapter, I have added additional resource suggestions to help you on your journey. Much of the resources are geared toward you as a parent to continue discovery, but there are some materials that are suggested reading for your child as well, and, in that case, I will note the age range next to the resource. You can certainly apply this section of the book and start shaping kingdom worldview concepts in your nations at any age.

CHAPTER 9

SETTING THE TABLE

"No man can live without a worldview; therefore, there is no man who is not a philosopher." – **Francis Schaeffer**

What's for dinner? A question that has been asked of me a minimum of 15,000 times in the past twenty-five years of parenting. Each week I meal plan; carefully balancing proteins, creativity, and flavors. I do my best to take into consideration the likes and dislikes of my family members and adjusting portions according to everyone's most current season of life. There have been seasons when I am creating new dishes two to three times per week, exposing my family to rich culture and flavors... And there have darn well been seasons when all I've had in me to cook were hotdogs and mac-and-cheese, with the occasional frozen pizza. I've learned to trust the Lord and embrace it all. Regardless of which meals I am planning, I have specifically found crafting my grocery list to be like solving an ever-evolving puzzle; one week I buy one gallon of milk, and it is gone in two days, so the next week I buy two gallons then suddenly, and unbeknownst to me, nobody likes milk, so both gallons go bad. Truly a first-world problem, I know, so I exercise gratefulness that my children are alive, healthy, and growing and begin again the next week attempting to crack the code. Such a seemingly small task of life consumes a large part of my time and energy each week as the keeper of my home, and I've come to appreciate the prophetic picture in meal planning, making dinner, and feeding my family.

The importance of exposing our children to all types of vegetables, fruits, proteins, and carbohydrates is highly recognized in our physical health world as of utmost importance. Creating a wide palate of taste gives our children opportunities to discover real and nourishing foods and teaches them how to be aware of and care for their bodies. By setting the dinner table with variety and depth, we give them enough room to cultivate a healthy lifestyle, which will translate to their quality and strength of engagement in the physical world. Just as we put so much time and effort into readying their physical bodies for the world, we must also learn to set the table and ready our nations in their spirit and soul (mind, will, and emotions) to engage with the world around them.

> "FOR BODILY TRAINING IS JUST SLIGHTLY BENEFICIAL, BUT GOD-LINESS IS BENEFICIAL FOR ALL THINGS, SINCE IT HOLDS PROMISE FOR THE PRESENT LIFE AND ALSO FOR THE LIFE TO COME."
> **– 1 TIMOTHY 4:8**

Your nations were born for this moment in history. Their life and existence are not a mistake. God looked down the corridor of time and saw fit for them to be alive in this day and for this dispensation, because He has placed something inside of them that will bring answers to the issues of the world around them. God has situated a key inside of your children that must be released to the world for the advancement of the gospel; to bring hope to the lost, healing to the broken, and freedom to the bound and oppressed. It is up to you to set the table of spiritual discovery and it's up to them to sit at that table, ask good questions, and seek God with all of their heart in each season. This is God's message to all of us, and this is the message I encourage you to pass onto your nations as you help them shape a kingdom worldview!

WHAT IS A WORLDVIEW?

I love puzzles. My favorites are the five-hundred-piece puzzles, because they can be done in a few hours or a day at the most. Usually, my family members will crowd around me and help; some for just a few minutes, some until the bitter end, and then there's that one kid of mine who likes to sneak a piece into his pocket, disappear for the duration of the puzzle, and then show up to put the last piece in for the finish. However we each choose to contribute, it's usually a great time of connection, problem solving, and conversation. We start by pouring the pieces out onto the table and begin putting the edge together carefully. Then we move on to the center sections, and at this point most of us will get stuck and grab the box cover to look at the picture. We then pass that cover around as each person needs. The cover reveals the bigger picture, so that when the pieces seem unclear or the pattern makes no sense, we can rely on the full image to guide our direction to the finish. If we had not been given the full picture on the box, we would each interpret the individual pieces differently from one another, quite likely incorrectly as well. Knowing the bigger picture helps us to interpret and respond to piece placement correctly. This is what it means to have a worldview; it's shaping our children's understanding of the greater picture, giving them a truthful interpretation and response to everything they encounter in life, as well as answering the big questions we all must ask. Worldview is the starting point for the decisions your children will make and the actions they will take in life.

Worldview has a two-part lens; it's interpretive and missional. It's our view *of* the world: how we <u>interpret</u> information, life situations, and relationships. It's also our view *for* the world; how we are on a <u>mission</u> to engage the cultures of the world around us, bringing the kingdom gospel of Jesus Christ. Shaping our nation's worldview is helping them understand how to perceive life and the purpose of the kingdom, as well as helping them discover how they are uniquely gifted to contribute to it. The apostle Peter assures us that the source of our worldview is found in God alone, "HIS DIVINE POWER HAS GRANTED TO US ALL THINGS THAT PERTAIN TO LIFE AND GODLINESS, THROUGH THE KNOWLEDGE OF HIM WHO CALLED US TO HIS OWN GLORY AND EXCELLENCE." - **2 Peter 1:3**

Shaping worldview means we must raise our nations with the understanding that ideas have consequences—and though our God is merciful, just, and kind—their choices will affect their quality of life and the life of those they are assigned to reach for the kingdom. Shaping a worldview takes time; it's not done overnight or in a one-dimensional teaching lesson, it takes intentionality, patience, surrender, and grace. A kingdom worldview provides meaning to life, and, as much of our attention as this may take for a season, rest assured that raising our children to understand how to think rightly about God and the world around them will give vast opportunities for them to influence the ideas that rule the culture.

EVERYONE HAS A WORLDVIEW

Nihilism, Transcendentalism, Theism, Spiritism, Naturalism... If you have a brain, you have a worldview, and it's innate for us to want to share our perception of life and circumstance with others. Take the various forms of media in our current day culture; social media, commercials, TV series, song lyrics, it couldn't be any clearer this day in age that everything has a message, and every message has an intended worldview to share. Now, I know this is where some might think, *"So, I'll just move into the country, homeschool, and never allow my kids to have a phone or a T.V. and pretend like the world doesn't exist."* Look, we homeschool, we've always tried to use wisdom in limiting device usage and conflicting environments, yet I personally don't subscribe to the belief that restricting our children's exposure to the world's messages means that they'll never be impacted by them. Rather, I believe in intentionally guiding our nations to understand that they indeed have a worldview to shape and so does everyone else, and I believe that this mindset will help them stay aware of the messages that are being sent to them through various platforms. Additionally, teaching them how to discern and rightly divide truth and talk about it will help them meet these oppositional messages head on and speak truth where there are lies. Friends, we are not raising escape-artists, we are raising nations that will confront the darkness and overcome it with Light in Jesus name!

> "AND DO NOT BE CONFORMED TO THIS WORLD [ANY LONGER WITH ITS SUPERFICIAL VALUES AND CUSTOMS], BUT BE TRANSFORMED AND PROGRESSIVELY CHANGED [AS YOU MATURE SPIRITUALLY] BY THE RENEWING OF YOUR MIND [FOCUSING ON GODLY VALUES AND ETHICAL ATTITUDES], SO THAT YOU MAY PROVE [FOR YOURSELVES] WHAT THE WILL OF GOD IS, THAT WHICH IS GOOD AND ACCEPTABLE AND PERFECT [IN HIS PLAN AND PURPOSE FOR YOU]" – **ROMANS 12:2 (AMP)**

THE TREE

Our worldview functions much like the beautiful tree described in **Psalm 1:1-3**, "HOW BLESSED IS THE MAN WHO DOES NOT WALK IN THE COUNSEL OF THE WICKED, NOR STAND IN THE PATH OF SINNERS, NOR SIT IN THE SEAT OF SCOFFERS! BUT HIS DELIGHT IS IN THE LAW OF THE LORD, AND IN HIS LAW, HE MEDITATES DAY AND NIGHT. HE WILL BE LIKE A TREE FIRMLY PLANTED BY STREAMS OF WATER, WHICH YIELDS ITS FRUIT IN ITS SEASON AND ITS LEAF

DOES NOT WITHER; AND IN WHATEVER HE DOES, HE PROSPERS." The three parts to a worldview are the roots, trunk, and branches. The roots are your theology: what you believe about God. The trunk is your philosophy: what is true and how you study truth. Then there are the branches which are the various mountains of influence in the world: psychology, sociology, politics, economy, biology, etc. These three parts function from the roots up; our children's theology (what they believe about God) will influence how they filter truth, and thus produce the fruit in their lives. The Psalmist says that when we meditate on the law of the Lord we will be planted by His streams of water, and we will produce fruit in season. Oftentimes we want to make a lot of fuss about changing the fruit we see coming through our kids—their attitudes, behaviors, philosophies, words, and mindsets—but if you want to change the fruit, you've got to deal with the roots! We will explore this in more depth a bit later in this chapter.

IMPORTANCE OF WORLDVIEWS

I came into my Worldview class on the first day and proposed a fundamental question to my students, *"Are you a Christian?"*

Multiple students confidently answered, *"Yes."*

"How do you know?", I asked.

"I grew up in a Christian home." "I go to church every week." "My parents are Christians." were among some of the answers I received. Not answers I expected to hear from teenagers growing up in Christian environments, and quite sobering to me as a mother of teens. I had to come to terms with the difference between being a kingdom example to my nations and encouraging them to come out from underneath my example and wrestle with their own faith before they embark on the journey into adulthood. *"Oftentimes it can be instinctive for us to believe that our worldview and beliefs are caught like a cold"*, I explained to my students, *"But, going to church doesn't make you a Christian, any more than being in a garage makes you a car."*

Worldview is an important structure of thought processes that help our children be in the world and not of it. It drives them to discern their purpose, hold the values of their identity, interpret God's will for now and eternity, and it fosters compassion in their hearts for those around them who are lost, hurting, and broken. We certainly do well to be an example of the kingdom to our nations and raise them in a kingdom environment, however they must be exhorted to grapple with and own their faith for themselves so that they can carry the torch into the world to others.

Operating on the defense and the offense are equally important; we must learn to defensively expose worldviews that oppose God's truth as well as train our children on the offense, to live out the truth of scripture in a culture hell-bent on denying it. George Barna, a well-known Christian statistician, did a youth poll on the spiritual activity of American teenagers and found that the percentage of teens engaged with church, bible reading, prayer, and sharing the gospel has been at a steady decline for decades, with only a mere 9% of teens who claim to be Christian say they believe in moral absolutes.[10] Bottom line is that our children are not immune to false cultural worldviews simply because they're raised in a Christian environment. If we want to successfully raise our nations for kingdom purpose, we must impart the discernment of scripture and train them to take the baton and continue to shape their worldview in Christ and Christ alone.

We are raising nations with a kingdom worldview that have the purpose to infiltrate every area of the world with the gospel of hope. Whether politics, economics, psychology, education, or any other branch of influence, everything is sacred to God, and His plan includes each one of us to partner with Him. There is a culture that stands above all cultures, races, classes, and distinctions; it is the kingdom culture. Jesus revealed the mystery of the kingdom in twelve parables listed in the gospels, and, because this kingdom has been revealed as countercultural and inverted to the way of the world, we must be intentional in cultivating a resolve in our nations to carry and defend it well. You can see why shaping worldview in and through our nations has high importance as they enter the world they are inheriting.

THE SHAPING OF A WORLDVIEW

As I mentioned in the previous pages, shaping a worldview is not done in a day, a month, or even a one-semester class. Shaping worldview means we must stay teachable and understand the times and seasons we live in today and the culture we will inherit tomorrow as it continues to change.

"In a world of change, the learners shall inherit the earth, while the learned shall find themselves perfectly suited for a world that no longer exists." **ERIC HOFFER**

Culture changes, it always has, and it will until the end of time, but why does it feel like it changes more rapidly today than ever before? We understand that cultural change is primarily driven by philosophical and technological advances. We also understand that we are experiencing as much technological progress in these current decades that many believe will amount to all that we've accomplished over the last several thousand years. That means cultural change is happening at a more rapid pace than ever before! I think of Justin and I raising our nations over the course of the last couple of decades, and, with the ten-year gap between our oldest and youngest, our four children have grown up in very different cultures as they've each entered young adulthood. Cell phones to smartphones, television to social media, radio to streaming, politics, social issues, online learning, it's all played a part into how we've had to adjust our parenting impact and help each of our children stay teachable as they shape their worldview and address the issues of the current time and season of culture.

> "BLESSED ARE THE MEEK, FOR THEY SHALL INHERIT THE EARTH."
> — MATTHEW 5:5

CONFRONTATION

The Greek word for meek in Matthew's scripture here is *praus*, which translates as humble. One of the ways writers have expounded on the idea of this Greek word, *praus*, is that it was used in the ancient military to define a horse trained for battle. Sam Whatley noted the following in an article he wrote for *River Regions Journey*...

> Wild stallions were brought down from the mountains and broken for riding. Some were used to pull wagons, some were raced, and the best were trained for warfare. They retained their fierce spirit, courage, and power, but were disciplined to respond to the slightest nudge or pressure of the rider's leg. They could gallop into battle at 35 miles an hour and come to a sliding stop at a word. They were not frightened by arrows, spears, or torches. Then they were said to be "meeked." To be "meeked" was to be taken from a state of wild rebellion and made completely loyal to, and dependent upon, one's master. It is also to be taken from an atmosphere of fearfulness and made unflinching in the presence of danger. Some war horses dove from ravines into rivers in pursuit of their quarry. Some charged into the face of exploding cannons as Lord Tennyson expressed in his poem, "The Charge of the Light Brigade." These stallions became submissive, but certainly not spineless. They embodied power under control, strength with forbearance.[11]

In biblical context, to be meek is often more focused on maintaining a position of submission and humility to God, and I love that Sam's interpretation of the war horse serves as a reminder that being humble does not mean we are spineless and tolerant of evil. The gospel is highly confrontational, the cross is offensively radical, and, although Jesus was indeed humble, His kingdom worldview did not tolerate evil... ever.

> *"When we truly believe the gospel, we begin to realize that the gospel not only compels Christians to confront social issues in the culture around us. The gospel actually creates confrontation with the culture around—and within us."*
> **– David Platt, Counterculture**

Lord, help us raise our nations to stand upon the Rock with confidence *and* humility, to not be conformed to the patterns of this world but to be transformed **(Romans 12:2)**, to possess power with submission to Christ and strength with forbearance. Shaping a worldview requires us to prepare our children to engage culture, confront the darkness, and allow the Holy Spirit to move through them to bring the hope of the gospel to a lost and dying world.

THE FUNCTION OF A WORLDVIEW

If we refer back to the tree that I mentioned earlier, we remember that our worldview has a three-fold function: **the roots, trunk, and branches.** These three functions work in succession to produce the fruit in our children's lives, both small and large pictures. Let's tackle this three-fold function of the worldview tree one bite at a time, starting with the roots, moving up to the trunk, and finally, to the branches.

THE ROOTS = THEOLOGY

The roots are the supply source to the tree, which is *theology*: your knowledge of God. Without the roots, a tree cannot live, let alone flourish or produce fruit. The roots anchor the tree in the soil to provide stability in harsh weather and nourishment to every part. Every bit of the fruit of your child's worldview and life will be drawn from their roots, which is the foundation of their theology: what they know and believe about God. This is the most important function of the worldview, and it cultivates a strong, healthy perspective.

> *"If man wants to change his behavior, he must first change the God he serves."*

Genesis 1:27 reveals that we are made in the image of God, thus what our children believe about God will translate to what they believe about themselves and others. Who they become is directly related to who they believe God to be. If your child sees God as controlling and critical, they may become angry and rebellious. If they believe God is indifferent or distant, they may rely on their own works to please Him, possibly developing dysfunctional attachment styles to Him and to people. Contrarily, if they know God as a loving Father, they will feel safe and confident to receive the kingdom like a child. If they believe God is merciful and forgiving, they will live their life in pursuit of a closeness to Him, because they feel accepted, even when they're at their worst. We will dive deeper into the question, *"Is God real? How do we know?"* in the next chapter, but the point I'm making is that the ultimate goal of shaping worldview is to cultivate true worshippers. The reality is not that our children can choose whether they will worship or not, but that they will indeed worship someone or something, and we must help guide them in choosing Who that will be. When they are firmly anchored in the roots of right belief in who God is, it will properly position their discernment of truth, which is the trunk of our worldview tree.

THE TRUNK = PHILOSOPHY

The trunk of the worldview tree is considered to be the filter of truth, or our *philosophy*; the study of what is true and how we know. We were created in truth and for truth! Raising our nations to discern and rightly divide truth will be the filter that separates the contaminants of duplicity and carries the nourishment of their theology to the fruit of their beliefs. They will be inundated with the abundance of opinions and information in our world, and it will either help them reinforce the fruit of truth or tear their beliefs apart with the rot of deception, so they must learn to discern truth. There are ways that we can engage with our children to teach them the process of filtering the information and messages of the world and limit the influence that it has in their soul. We want our children to fully develop an understanding of how to study what is true, reason with reality, and stay anchored in Christ.

SEEKING AND STUDYING TRUTH

I've heard it said that truth does not deny the seeker. Jesus clarifies the source of truth by declaring, "I AM THE WAY, THE TRUTH, AND THE LIFE; NOBODY COMES TO THE FATHER EXCEPT BY ME." **(John 14:6)** If we want to understand what is true, we must seek Jesus. When we become lovers of wisdom and seekers of truth, we will first open our hearts to know God and be known by Him because He is the truth. Jesus prayed for us, "SANCTIFY THEM BY THE TRUTH; YOUR WORD IS TRUTH." **(John 17:17)**, the word of God sanctifies our hearts and routes out the deception that can get tangled in our mindsets. Sometimes being a truth-seeker means you need to let go of emotional attachments that you have to your personal opinions and beliefs. Let's encourage our nations to remain teachable seekers of truth in Christ, there is always something more to learn about Him and the world around us!

When my kids were little, they loved to drink out of my water bottle. Look, I share and have shared most things with my kids; my body, my clothes, my bed, my food, and my personal space, but something I was not a fan of was sharing drinks with my back-washing-runny-nosed toddlers. Just not into it. So, when my kids were toddlers, I would keep my water bottle up high and out of their reach. Our youngest, David, was and is an incredibly tenacious and driven young man and, no matter where I would place my water, he would always find it and sneak drinks from it when I wasn't looking. One afternoon I was standing in the kitchen, cleaning off the laminated maps that we used for geography, while he was cruising around with his trucks, playing independently. I had a bottle of rubbing alcohol on the center island counter that I was using to clean the maps and I had left the cap off to make the task more efficient. As I inspected one of the maps with my back facing the island, I heard a *gurgle, cough, choke,* and finally a very angry cry. I turned around to see David perched on the bar stool with the bottle of rubbing alcohol in his hands staring at me as if it was personal. He had mistaken the clear liquid in the bottle as a refreshing drink of water but had another thing coming. I have never had to call poison control for any of my other children, just my sweet David. I explained the situation to the lady on the phone, and she determined that David likely didn't drink enough to cause alarm, so she instructed me to give him some milk and a cookie to coat his stomach and keep his blood sugars up until it passed through. All was well and peace was restored in the home once again. Had David known to investigate the truth about the clear liquid lurking in that bottle, I can't help but think he would have made a different choice. If he'd known it was rubbing alcohol and not water, he may have decided against it. It was a good life lesson for him to slow down and discern truth before ingesting anything, and it wouldn't be the last time I would guide my nations through the process of investigating truth before consuming. Being a truth-seeker is a foundational part of our identity as kingdom citizens, and raising our nations to love truth, seek truth, and study what is true in a world full of lies will set them apart and set them up for successful impact.

> Do your best to present yourself to God as one approved, a worker who does not need to be ashamed and who correctly handles the word of truth. – **2 Timothy 2:15**

THE END OF REASON

"Because I said so" is a frequent response of parents with children, especially small children who are in the, *"but, why?"* phase of the journey. This phrase sums up the end of our parental efforts to give answers to the reasons why we do what we do. It's instinctive for any human, but especially little humans, to want to understand the reason for the decisions that are made, especially when those decisions impact them personally. As your nations grow into middle schoolers and teens, they will with certainty ask you questions about life and God that you cannot answer, and you may be tempted to pull some version of the *"because I said so"* card out of your back pocket, maybe out of fear, or perhaps because you're just tired of admitting you don't have answers. Instead, I encourage you to lean into the questions your highschoolers present to you, admit when you don't know, and let it drive you to dive deeper for yourself! In regard to our faith, the Apostle Peter instructs us to know why we believe what we believe (**1 Peter 3:15**), and when we reach the end of reason, we are urged to walk by faith with confidence in the things we cannot see or understand

using the conviction of the spirit **(2 Corinthians 5:7)**. As we raise our nations, we want them to develop a personal conviction of their belief in God while also recognizing that it's not enough for them to believe what is true based on personal conviction alone. The world is searching for truth, and when our children begin to share the hope of the gospel, people will ask, *"but why?"* It's imperative we give our nations the tools to rightly seek, study, and divide truth, so that they can heed the words of the Apostle Peter and give answers for the hope they have.

> "BUT SANCTIFY CHRIST AS LORD IN YOUR HEARTS, ALWAYS BEING READY TO MAKE A DEFENSE TO EVERYONE WHO ASKS YOU TO GIVE AN ACCOUNT FOR THE HOPE THAT IS IN YOU, BUT WITH GENTLENESS AND RESPECT." - **1 PETER 3:15**

The following are five main methods of studying truth that we can use to help guide our children on the journey of shaping the trunk of their philosophy:

1. **Appealing to Authority** – Primary and secondary sources such as eyewitness accounts and historical documents are ways that we can prove historical events and teach them as truth. For example, none of us were at the scene of Abraham Lincoln's assassination, yet we believe it happened because we have read historical documents and eyewitness accounts of the event. There are multiple documents and eyewitness accounts that prove Jesus' life, death, and resurrection are true, the Bible is not the only source, but certainly key among them. Teach your growing teens to read the Word, love the Word, study the Word, and know the Word in depth so that they can give an account for the hope that is in them.

2. Reason – Reasoning is something that many Christians argue has no place in the realm of faith, but God has a different opinion in **Isaiah 1:18,** "Come now, let us reason together, says the Lord..." To reason simply means to argue or debate with <u>common sense</u> or natural logic and it works beautifully with faith. God gave us a brain for a good purpose; common sense reveals truth in simple questions like *can a person be a married bachelor? If I touch the hot stove, will I get burned? Does 2+2=3? Will I die someday?* There are two common misconceptions about truth that are widely accepted in culture today. The first one is that if we believe something to be true then it's true, but if I believe that 2+2=3, would that make it true? The second misconception is that truth is not absolute, it's relative to our preference and we each live our truth. The challenge with both of these statements is that in order for them to be true there has to be absolute truth that proves it! You can see why common-sense reasoning is an important detector of truth. Teaching our nations how to think, reason, and use common sense is a natural path that encourages the exploration of truth. Where reason ends, faith begins!

3. Conscience – In the heart of every human there is a conscience, or intuition knowledge of right and wrong. Without being told, humanity has always known that it is wrong to kill an innocent human being—that's not to say that some humans don't care that it's wrong, just that inherently we know it's wrong. Even Cain knew it was wrong to kill his brother, Abel, though he didn't have the ten commandments telling him that it was wrong. Conscience is something God placed inside each one of us as a compass to discern what is true, just, and right; it's that gut feeling. The Apostle Paul shares that our conscience can hold us in bondage to religion, "THEY SHOW THAT THE WORK OF THE LAW IS WRITTEN ON THEIR HEARTS, WHILE THEIR CONSCIENCE ALSO BEARS WITNESS, AND THEIR CONFLICTING THOUGHTS ACCUSE OR EVEN EXCUSE THEM" **- Romans 2:15**. Our conscience can lead us to intimate knowledge of God, " FOR GOD, WHO SAID, "LET LIGHT SHINE OUT OF DARKNESS," HAS SHONE IN OUR HEARTS TO GIVE THE LIGHT OF THE KNOWLEDGE OF THE GLORY OF GOD IN THE FACE OF JESUS CHRIST." **- 2 Corinthians 4:6**. When our conscience is ignored, over time we can become desensitized to the warnings of corruption, so teaching our nations to be tenderly aware of their conscience will help keep them sensitive to God's voice and the guidance of His Spirit.

4. Practical Experience – There is this plastic red and blue ball that all of my kids played with when they were babies, it had multiple holes all around it with various-shaped openings. It came with the yellow shapes to fit into the proper openings, and the intent was to teach them practical experience with matching shapes together. Naturally they learned that the yellow star shape doesn't fit into the round hole, and the yellow square shape doesn't fit into the triangle-shaped opening; they learned this by practical experience. Now that they are older, they know that they cannot use an Allen wrench to turn a flathead screw, or boil water in the freezer simply because it can be tested with practical experience. This is how we explore the truth of scientific concepts as well. Likely you've applied this learning technique to your younger babies and toddlers, therefore learning with hands-on experience is not necessarily a new concept as your children become teenagers, but it still holds great value! Being intentional to give your teens space for trial and error and then drawing out the lessons through success and failure will show them how to use practical experience to understand truth on a larger scale. Don't be afraid to let them learn by trial and error!

5. **Personal Encounter** – At first glance this seems redundant to practical experience, however personal encounter is specifically about guiding your children to connect with God on a personal level. It's about moving beyond a head knowledge of God and teaching them to root themselves in personal encounters with Jesus and to linger in the presence of the Holy Spirit. I continue to pray for each of my kids to radically encounter Jesus for themselves, because I realized many years ago that their faith will suffer a shipwreck if they rely on my devotion to Christ to be their anchor. They must know Him intimately and encounter the Holy Spirit for themselves. I gave each one of my nations a prophetic journal when they were young, and I began teaching them how to tune into what God was showing or speaking to them, encouraging them to ask God a question and write down what they heard Him say or draw out what they saw. I have fond and precious memories of reading their entries and watching them learn to capture God's heart. I specifically remember the lengthy explanations that five-year-old David would give me because he didn't know how to spell quite yet so he would draw abstract pictures of what he saw in his imagination. As they've grown through the seasons of questioning God's reality, they refer back often to those moments that God showed up to them personally. When your children understand Him with reason, and then encounter Him personally, an unshakable and lasting foundation is built in their hearts that will withstand the storms of life.

These are just a few ways that we can encourage our nations to seek and study truth, carefully investigating before they consume what the culture dishes up. Knowing how to study and discern truth will carry the lifeblood of faith to the branches of our worldview tree.

> "SO THAT CHRIST MAY DWELL IN YOUR HEARTS THROUGH FAITH; AND THAT YOU, BEING ROOTED AND GROUNDED IN LOVE, MAY BE ABLE TO COMPREHEND WITH ALL THE SAINTS WHAT IS THE WIDTH AND LENGTH AND HEIGHT AND DEPTH, AND TO KNOW THE LOVE OF CHRIST WHICH SURPASSES KNOWLEDGE, THAT YOU MAY BE FILLED TO ALL THE FULLNESS OF GOD." – **EPHESIANS 3:17-19**

Extra Philosophy Resources:

- *"Halfway Herbert"* by Francis Chan (for ages 4-8)
- *"Fallacy Detective"* by Nathaniel Bluedorn (6th-12th grade)
- *"The Pattern of God's Truth"* by Frank Gaebelein (Homeschool parent resource)

THE BRANCHES = SPHERES OF INFLUENCE

The worldview tree is stabilized in the roots of theology, filtered through the trunk of philosophy, and carried to the branches of influence which include but are not limited to marriage, family, church, community, ministry, politics, law, economics, history, psychology, and so much more. Essentially, every human is in relationship with God, themselves, and all of creation, so the secondary lens of helping our nations shape their worldview is to connect them in relationship to the Lord and prepare them for the influence they will have in the world. Because the branches of influence are vast, we could fill multiple chapters exploring and breaking down a kingdom worldview in each branch, and while I don't intend to do that in this book (maybe that will be my next book), there are limitless resources that you can use to be successful on this journey!

Justin and I have personally chosen to homeschool all four of our children, and for twenty years we have been able to thoughtfully choose curriculums in each branch of influence to help shape their worldview. You certainly do not have to be a homeschooler to accomplish the goal of kingdom worldview in branches like biology, politics, and sociology, but I would encourage you to be very involved with your child's education in whatever capacity you are able, so you can help guide their thought process as they discern truth in each area. As our nations have grown into teenagers and young adults, each one of them has discovered their gifts and developed God-given passions for different branches of influence in the world, and each one of them is so very different in how they walk out that mission. Maiya has a heart for local community programming, Evelyn has had intrigue for the world of psychology and medicine, Matthew is on course for influencing the nutrition industry, and David has his sights set on leading the domain of business. You too will find that it's not a one-size-fits-all journey with your kids, and I encourage you to pray that God will help you excavate their unique gifts to share with the world. There is no separation between sacred and secular, God cares about the natural and supernatural worlds, and He invites us all into partnership with Him in carrying out His plans. We will dive further into the topic of purpose and assignments *(why am I here?)* in a later chapter.

Extra Branch Curriculum Resources:

- *www.apologia.com*
- *www.sonlight.com*
- *www.the101series.com*
- *www.compassclassroom.com*

SET THE TABLE

Imagine inviting friends over for dinner and you've got the tablescape set with warm candles, beautiful bowls, polished serving platters, and crystal glasses buffed to a clear shine. But when your company comes over, they sit down to find the bowls empty and the platters with a layer of dust. They leave hungry, disappointed, and maybe a bit disgusted. The table setting creates the expectation that there is substance being served and care put into the meal. As we are shaping our children, it's not enough to create polished personalities or sparkling behavior, but we must teach them how to cultivate substance within, so that they can be an arm of provision to those around them who will come hungry to know the truth. Let us bring our children up to be holy vessels and raise them with a worldview that will impact the nations!

> "WOE TO YOU, SCRIBES AND PHARISEES, HYPOCRITES! FOR YOU CLEAN THE OUTSIDE OF THE CUP AND OF THE DISH, BUT INSIDE THEY ARE FULL OF ROBBERY AND SELF-INDULGENCE." – **MATTHEW 23:25**

Extra Worldview Resources:

- *"Faith for Exiles"* by David Kinnamann
- *"Counterculture"* by David Platt
- *"How to be Your Own Selfish Pig"* by Susan Schaeffer Macaulay (6th-12th grade)
- *"The Consequences of Ideas"* by R.C. Sproul

PRAYER

Father, thank you for being the ultimate example of kingdom worldview. I receive the abundance of grace and the gift of righteousness that I would reign in this life by Christ Jesus and likewise help shape the reigning kingdom worldview in my nations. I acknowledge and accept that I am not Jesus, and I cannot create a worldview for my kids, but I can show them the way to the One who can. I choose to partner with your will and design for their lives and ask you to lead me by your Spirit on this journey. Search my heart and lay the foundation of kingdom worldview in me before I attempt to promote it in them. Let all we perceive of the world and resolve to do in the world be centered in you and for your glory in Jesus' name, AMEN!!

REFLECTION/DISCUSSION QUESTIONS

1. Where do I need to start shaping a kingdom worldview in my own perception of the world and my mission for the world?

2. What is one thing I can start doing to develop the roots of theology in my kids?

3. What is one thing I can start doing to encourage my nations in the process of learning how to discern truth?

4. How can I begin praying right now for the hearts to be prepared for shaping a kingdom worldview?

CHAPTER 10

SO MANY QUESTIONS!

"The master key of knowledge is, indeed,
*a persistent and frequent questioning." – **Peter Abelard***

Have you ever felt "crusty" in your faith? You know, it's that stale, stagnant, bored, or cynical feeling. Maybe you used to pore over scriptures with wonder and excitement, and now reading the bible has lost its zest. Maybe you once attended church services for five hours and it felt like five minutes and now a 40-minute sermon feels too long and all you pull out of it is the handful of grammatical errors the pastor spoke. Perhaps the church has hurt you, and now you're more of a spectator with a fear of getting too close to community, which in turn makes you feel alone. When I said yes to Jesus at age 22, I was ON FIRE! Everything was new, exhilarating, wondrous, and life-altering. I was diving into topics such as righteousness, healing, eternity, and forgiveness. Justin and I would set up meeting after meeting with our pastor to ask questions about life: *why did God create us? What happens when we die? What about sin and sickness?* The pastor would answer some of our questions directly and then give us book recommendations for some personal discovery of the others. I have to smile when I think back now at how elementary the questions were that I asked in the beginning. I had not grown up in church, so

143

it was all new and fascinating to me. After about a year and a half I started noticing I was losing my gusto to pursue deeper depths; prayer seemed hard, my eyes were heavy when I read the Bible; my faith was secure and my hope fixed in Jesus, but it fell a little flat. Anyone who knows me knows that I'm not one to do anything halfway, or out of obligation, so this disposition was very bothersome to me. As I sat in my living room chair one afternoon to pray and read the bible while my babies napped, I started to complain to God about feeling stale and uninterested. *"Seek and you'll find"*, I felt the nudge of the Holy Spirit addressing the issue, I had stopped asking good questions. I lost my childlike hunger for discovery. Thinking I'd learned quite a bit, I got too satisfied to feast off of the past season's discoveries, and now I was chewing on bones. I needed a fresh revelation; I needed to start asking deeper questions to discover more of God. It seems simple, but questions are truly the driving force of growth and that's all it took for my feet to get off the ground again. After twenty-one years of walking with Jesus I can honestly say that I've hit a few of these "crusty" seasons; I'll start leaning into the busy, cynical, or plain disinterested attitudes, and find myself pulling away from the body of believers. I can now recognize the seasons when they come and, instead of letting an indifferent disposition linger or get me stuck, I repent of an attitude of knowing-it-all and begin to press into the new with good questions for the Lord to reveal Himself.

> "IF ANYONE THINKS THAT HE KNOWS ANYTHING, HE HAS NOT YET KNOWN AS HE OUGHT TO KNOW." – **1 CORINTHIANS 8:2**

When my teens began to ask hard questions about God, faith, life, religion, and the case for Jesus, it didn't bother me, it excited me, because I remember the times of my own growth and discovery by way of asking good questions. However, I have come to find that some parents, especially parents who have spent their whole life in church, are quite fearful of their teens asking questions. I've had parents contact me regarding their student suddenly having too many questions about their faith in God after week four of taking my Worldview class and they want to know what's going on! I constantly reassure them that questions are absolutely necessary for the longevity of faith, as scary as it is, and that their teens are quite capable of taking this journey with the Lord. I think there are a few reasons why we as parents can be fearful and avoidant of questions. Sometimes our nations' questions can be confrontational to our lack of ownership of our own faith, and we realize we've not asked good questions for personal growth. Perhaps our pride is bruised to admit we don't have all of the answers and cannot be the superhero we want to be for our teens. But most often it's because we might interpret the asking of questions as doubt, and, since doubt and faith seemingly cannot co-exist, it is frowned upon to ask hard questions. We see this play out especially in very religious circles. When we search the scriptures, we find that faith in the New Testament was driven by questions, questions that sought to break the masses out of the rut of religion and restore them to freedom in relational discovery.

I wholeheartedly believe that great disciples ask good questions, and I find it fascinating that while the people asked many questions of Jesus, Jesus also asked an incredible number of questions of the people—it was one of His primary teaching styles. In the season of learning to own their faith, your nations will desire to ask many hard questions. Fear not! Relax and let God unfold the beautiful mess of discovery, but also remember that you can draw out their process with your own good questions too. Questions like, *"What do you think about (kingdom topic)?" "What is God showing you right now?" "What is challenging for you in this season of your faith?" "What is not making sense to you?"* will open the doors for great discussion and growth opportunities for them AND you! Remember that every time you ask a question you open a gate to the path of discovery, and every time you make a statement, you close that gate for your child. Let us encourage our middle school and highschoolers to ask good questions, hard questions, weird questions, any questions, so that there is fuel in their tank to move forward in their faith. Likewise, let us follow in the footsteps of Jesus and ask good questions of our nations as they cross the threshold of discovery, helping them position their hearts to receive fresh revelation in every season of life!

FOUR ULTIMATE QUESTIONS

As we've discovered, there are so many questions to ask! Worldview is often broken down into what is named the "four ultimate questions", which are foundational for humans to navigate this life and the life to come. *Where did I come from? Why am I here? How do I live? Where do I go when I die?* Are among the burning questions on the hearts of every human starting at the middle school/high school age. I typically spend fourteen of the twenty-eight weeks of my Worldview class each year teaching on these four ultimate questions, so, for the sake of brevity and the prevention of boredom, I do not intend to expound in full length on any of these four questions, I only hope to shed some light on the path and leave the rest of the discovery up to you!

There are a multitude of ways that these four questions can be categorized and taught, but I've chosen to compile them into an expression of **Ephesians 2:10**, when Paul begins to describe us each as God's workmanship. The word workmanship in the Greek is *poiema,* and it's where we get our English word, *poem.* We are a beautiful piece of poetry crafted by God; He has chosen us before the foundations of the earth, He has purposed us, He has given us direction and a final destination with Him, therefore, I thought it fitting to break these four very important questions of life down in an easy to remember format, with the acronym P.O.E.M.: purpose, origins, eternity, morality. Now the only downside of this acronym is that it doesn't list these ultimate questions in order of life process—beginning, middle, end—but I have found that human beings, and most prominently our children, don't necessarily ask these questions in order of life process. In fact, typically the first question to get asked is, *"Why am I here?"* which, as Divine providence would have it, happens to be the first question in the acronym, so... (insert shoulder shrug emoji).

> "WE HAVE BECOME HIS POETRY, A RE-CREATED PEOPLE THAT WILL FULFILL THE DESTINY HE HAS GIVEN EACH OF US, FOR WE ARE JOINED TO JESUS, THE ANOINTED ONE. EVEN BEFORE WE WERE BORN, GOD PLANNED IN ADVANCE OUR DESTINY AND THE GOOD WORKS WE WOULD DO TO FULFILL IT!" – **EPHESIANS 2:10 (TPT)**

P - PURPOSE OF LIFE

"Why am I here?" "What is my purpose?" "What is the meaning of life?"

As I mentioned, this question is often the first and probably the most frequently asked among the ultimate questions of life. Every one of us has a longing to understand why our individual life is important, and if what we do even matters in the grand scheme of things. Each life is a unique part of the overall plan of God on the earth. Each person's life has meaning, first of all to be in relationship with God and then to partner with Him and carry the kingdom to the world. As your middle or high school nations walk the journey of owning their faith, the question of purpose is an ever lingering one, simply because it takes time to personally discover the details of their design. I interpret individual purpose as a two-fold function: motivation and mission. Motivation is about what moves us into action, are you motivated by practical needs to be filled? Is it someone who needs encouragement that moves you? Is it a problem to be solved?

Or perhaps information that needs to be understood? The Apostle Paul breaks these unique motivations down in Romans 12 as the Grace Gifts. The grace gifts consist of seven basic motivational wirings: *Prophecy, Service, Teaching, Exhortation, Giving, Administration, and Mercy*. We have more free resources for discovery on this topic on our website, which I've listed under the resource section. Feel free to explore and download anything that helps you on the journey. For now, I will list each motivational gift and the burning question this gift asks when it walks into a room.

- **Prophecy** – What are the hidden issues that need to come to light?
- **Serving** – Where are the needs and how can I help?
- **Teaching** – How can I get informed and inform others?
- **Exhortation** – What is the goal and how can we achieve it?
- **Giving** – Where are the opportunities and how can I bring increase?
- **Administration** – What is the strategic plan and how will we execute?
- **Mercy** – Who is hurting and how can I help?

Whatever your nation's motivation, it is what propels them into the second part of their purpose, which is their personal mission. Their mission is their "why"—the goal of their action. *Why do I want to encourage others? Why do I want to show compassion? Why do I want to fill this need?* For example, if someone has a motivation of serving—to fill practical needs—they may discover that their mission in filling those needs is to bring things into order. I personally operate high in prophecy and exhortation motivations and my mission or "why" tends to be geared toward reformation along with cultivating more efficient and focused environments. The mission function of your teen's purpose will take a bit more time to articulate as they grow into adulthood because it's primarily understood through observation of their response in everyday life situations. It's great to get them to start thinking about it as they're maturing so they can dialogue with the Lord and step into their assignments with resolve in each season of life!

Extra Purpose Resources:

- www.occupy-freedom.com (Toolbox tab)
- *"The Search for Significance, Student Edition"* by Robert Mcgee (8th-12th grade)
- *"Amusing Ourselves to Death"* by Neil Postman

0 - ORIGINS

Where did it all come from? Does God exist?

Your life is not a mistake, God knew you before you were formed and before you were born. He has set your destiny in motion and has given you a purpose–a specific way that you will contribute to His overall plan on the earth. God has good works that He desires for you to walk in, so that your life will not just have a temporary meaning, but an eternal impact! In order to know where you're going and what your purpose is, it's first important to understand where you come from, where it began, and Who it began with. The real cry of our hearts when we ask where it all came from is, *"Is God real?"* There are two primary ways that this question is answered. The first is evolution: the theory that species evolved over time by random genetic mutation. The second is Design Theory, which holds that life and the universe are best explained by an intelligent cause. The real mission of evolutionary theory is to prove that God is not necessary for explaining life and meaning. When you talk with your nations about this question, the real grapple is whether or not God exists or if all that we see is just random mutated goo. It's vital to answer this question because if God is not real, then answering the follow-up question, *"what is my purpose"* drastically changes course. Because this topic is foundational to raising our nations, I've devoted the next chapter solely on how to break down the case for God's existence, how we know, and how it impacts us. There are many great resources on the topic of creation vs. evolution and I've included a couple of them below. I highly encourage you to have thorough debate and discussion around this question with your kids!

Extra Creation Resources:

- *"It Couldn't Just Happen"* by Lawrence Richards (6th-12th grade)
- www.answersingenesis.org   (Creation   and   Evolution resources)

E - ETERNITY

What happens when I die?

Death. A great topic to kill a party. We attended a wedding a few years ago and as the bride stood there in her beautiful dress, gazing into the eyes of her soon-to-be husband, the pastor spoke a twenty-minute message about death. Death? I was like, *"what in the morbid marital oppression is this?"* I had legit never heard of death being the topic of a wedding before, and I felt uncomfortable for the crowd for a few moments, but something the pastor said really struck me, *"You aren't just helping each other live well, you are committing to help each other die well."* Wow. What a sobering and profoundly beautiful reality that we are not just helping one another live successful lives here on earth, but more importantly we are helping each other die well by fixing our gaze upon eternity and being on mission so that when we move to the life here-after, we will hear, *"Well done, good and faithful servant!"* We might feel uncomfortable with our mortality or consider it morbid to talk about death, but we all share this beautiful guarantee in this life; we will all die one day. I know, you're loving this section already.

"Set your mind on things above, not on things on the
earth." – **Colossians 3:2**

It's not morbid for us to talk about dying, in fact it brings alignment to the spiritual reality that we don't belong to this world and
that our citizenship is in heaven (Chapter 1). Jesus had much to
say about the death of this life and the hope of the life to come; He
wasn't coming to set up His kingdom on earth, He was preaching
the gospel of eternity—the hope of the next life! I'm convinced
the reason why many people are plagued with anxiety and depression more and more is that we have our gaze so transfixed on this
temporal world: working hard to achieve comfort, build success,
protect our luxuries, and enjoy our freedoms, that when challenges
arise in any given arena, we fall to pieces worrying about the horizontal business of the world instead of meditating on the vertical
realities of eternity. Our anchors have become too heavily rooted
in what is happening to us in this world and how to live our best
life. While I am a firm believer in living a resurrection powered
life, I pray I would never forget the simple truth: that NOTHING
(marriages, finances, health, ministry, business, pleasures, family)
has meaning without God. Without Him nothing was made that
is made. The psalmist says it best, "THERE IS NOTHING UPON THE
EARTH THAT I DESIRE BESIDES THEE" - **Psalm 73:25**. When our
gaze is fixed on eternity, we become unbothered by the threats
of the temporary situations of life. Let us talk about the reality of
heaven with our nations, raise them to stay fixed on things above,
and to teach them to build here on earth with eternity in mind.
Because it's an inevitable part of our journey in life, it's perfectly
natural for us as humans to ponder death, and, instead of avoiding
the topic, we should encourage our children to process the certainty of death with the hope and truth of eternity in mind. Do you
understand what will happen when you die? Do you have your

eyes fixed upon eternity? Let's open the scriptures and help our nations understand the purpose of their life and what will happen when this chapter closes.

Some questions to spark conversation with your nations:
How do you feel about death?
What do you think happens when we die?
Do you have hope for eternity?
How does eternity change the way you want to live on earth?

Extra Eternity Resources:

- *"Tell me About Eternity"* by Joel Anderson (age 5-6 years)
- *"Heaven Awaits"* by Michael Youssef
- *"Stop Erasing Hell"* by Francis Chan & Preston Sprinkle
- *"Recapturing Eternity"* by Ralph Berry

M - MORALITY

"How should I live?" *"What is right and wrong and how do we know?"*

Most middle and highschoolers won't ask this question, rather, they tend to learn with observation and trial & error. Whether they voice this question or not, our nations will grapple with the concept of what is right and wrong as they transition into their mission in the world. Media, teachers, and influential relationships will constantly be throwing this question at them in subtle ways. *"What is right and wrong and how do I know?"* Many people believe that society decides what is the standard of right or wrong, and the group with the loudest voice in society will determine how we view moral issues such as the value of unborn life, sexuality, relationships, or personal behavior. If we search the globe, we will find a variety of moral standards in a multitude of different cultures; some cultures find it okay to steal as long as you don't get caught, others allow the molesting and sacrificing of children for religious purposes, and still other cultures operate in caste systems to organize the value of human life based on melanin levels. Morals also change depending on the century we live in or personal opinions, so it's no wonder the world's wisdom says morality is relative to personal preference and cultural acceptability. However, as kingdom citizens, we are to have an inverted view of morality from the norm of the world. Paul urges the Romans to not be conformed to the pattern of the world (**Romans 12:2**), Jesus prays for us to be in the world but not of it (**John 17:16**), and John exhorts that "NO ONE WHO HAS BEEN BORN OF GOD PRACTICES SIN, BECAUSE HIS SEED REMAINS IN HIM; AND HE CANNOT SIN CONTINUALLY, BECAUSE HE HAS BEEN BORN OF GOD." - **1 John 3:9**. Remember that the roots of our nations' theology create a sap that nourishes their whole worldview tree, and what they believe about God's view of morality will affect the moral fruit produced in every area of their lives. As believers, our source of morality and ethics—why and how we make moral choices—is found in God alone. Raising our nations to understand that morals are not relative but, rather, they are absolute, will set them up for unshakable fruit in a world of gray areas and unstable ideals.

> "I PRAY THAT YOU WILL CONTINUALLY EXPERIENCE THE IMMEASURABLE GREATNESS OF GOD'S POWER MADE AVAILABLE TO YOU THROUGH FAITH. THEN YOUR LIVES WILL BE AN ADVERTISEMENT OF THIS IMMENSE POWER AS IT WORKS THROUGH YOU!"
> – **EPHESIANS 1:90-20 (TPT)**

Another important key to help our nations understand is that they are a walking billboard for the glory of God; their life is ministry to the person sitting next to them in class, guarding them during basketball practice, and standing next to them in the Target checkout line. Jesus told His disciples in **Matthew 10** to GO and preach and that the kingdom of heaven was at hand, meaning that wherever their feet would tread, they would be bringing the kingdom to that space.

Our nations hold a powerful key piece to the larger plan of God, and the choices they make and the life that they live is not just a matter of personal consequences, it's a matter of building an eternal legacy!

Some of you might be reading this and thinking, *"what about being too legalistic about behavior?"* Excellent question, holiness is about embracing who you are in Christ and allowing your life to produce the fruit of your relationship with Him—remember the illustration of the pepper plant back in chapter seven? Religion is about embracing your works as a means to be in Him; you know you're being legalistic if you depend on behavior to define your relationship with God. If you push your nations to be good and moral because it's how you define the value of their faith and the validation of your parenting, then you're being legalistic. On the contrary, if you lead them to a right relationship with God and teach them that the fruit of their lives will bear witness out of love, you're teaching them holiness. Teaching our nations the full gospel requires us to lead them to the cross of repentance and then to the resurrection of new life and power.

"Right behavior does not produce right relationship, but right relationship WILL produce right behavior."
–Joyce Meyer

Extra Lifestyle Resources:

- *"How Should We Then Live?"* by Francis Schaeffer (9th-12th grade)
- *"How to be Your Own Selfish Pig"* by Susan Schaeffer Macaulay (8th-12th grade)

SO MANY QUESTIONS!

As we've discovered, good questions are imperative to the long-lasting development of every disciple, and that there will be many questions your nations will ask, and honestly, many you may not want to answer or discuss. It's also good to remember that they may not always think about or want to ask about some of these topics, so I encourage you to take initiative and get them thinking. Use the above four ultimate questions to start good conversations with your nations, you will not regret investing in this process of shaping worldview with them. I'll end this chapter with encouragement and reiteration from Chapter 2…

"With your children, opportunities for meaningful conversations may often come at very inconvenient times, but they hold the potential of priceless growth and influence. Meaningful conversations can be hard conversations, so you must be willing to yield yourself to uncomfortable topics and questions such as sexuality, questioning faith, stewarding possessions, drugs and alcohol, and personal struggles. I often lean into the concept of "The law of first mention" when it comes to hard topics like these. This principle is often used when studying the scriptures and it embraces the idea that if you want to understand the context of a particular word, imagery, or story, you must go back to where it was first mentioned in the Bible. As it pertains to your kids, you want to be the first mention: the first person to teach them the truth of life, love, kingdom, and cultural content, because this will set a proper reference point for them to come back to when they are faced with challenges in those areas."

Extra Worldview Resources:

- *Worldview Curriculum* for homeschooling – Summit Ministries, www.summit.org
- *"C.S. Lewis and the Christian Worldview"* by Michael Peterson
- *"Total Truth – Liberating Christianity from its Cultural Captivity"* by Nancy Pearcey

PRAYER

Jesus, thank you that you ask such great questions of each one of us to lead us in the way everlasting! Lord, thank you for an abundance of grace to ask and answer good questions of my nations. I want to embrace the questions of their process and allow it to both mature me and challenge me as well. I acknowledge and accept that I cannot answer all questions because I am not God, but I know the One who can, and I want to become a strong arrow to your throne. Holy Spirit, help guide me in the way of truth and build a strong connection between me and my kids as they open up and ask questions while they seek truth. Empower me to be an example of discipleship and holiness in every area of my life. In Jesus' name I pray, AMEN!

REFLECTION/DISCUSSION QUESTIONS:

1. What are some good questions I can start asking my kids in their current season of life?

2. What questions might my kids ask me that I feel ill-equipped to answer? How can I cultivate my kingdom worldview to be prepared to guide them?

3. What do I need to do to become a more effective listener of my children?

CHAPTER 11

FATHER, SON, AND HOLY SPIRIT

*The main problem with those who deny the existence of God
is not intellectual. It is not because of insufficient information,
or that God's manifestation of himself in nature has been obscured.
The atheist's problem is not that they cannot know God,
rather it is they do not want to know him. Man's problem
with the existence of God is not an intellectual problem;
it is a moral problem."*
– R. C. Sproul

If what we believe about God will ultimately determine what we believe about ourselves and the world we are called to impact, then it stands to reason for us to take time discovering the Father, Son, and Holy Spirit. Can we know if God is real? There is a rise in our culture today of what is called an "agnostic" worldview, this is defined by the belief that God's existence cannot be known—and I would add *"so carry on with your life how you wish."* It's true that we cannot prove with 100% certainty that God exists, but, after reading this chapter and discovering the overwhelming evidence, I think you may find that the agnostic worldview is motivated by a deeper desire to ignore the evidence for God, rather than investigate it and make a personal decision about it. As kingdom parents raising nations for God, I desire for us to be diligent to understand the case for God's existence, and to impart the mission of discovering who He is and what He is like. Taking time for thorough investigation and impartation in this area will be a key foundation to your nation's unshakable worldview.

DOES GOD EXIST?

This ultimate question is the axis on which all other questions can be answered, for without God's existence everything else changes its trajectory. "Does God exist?" is the underlying ache of each human's heart, it's the motivation for our search for significance, and it's the rudder to the ship we navigate in finding identity, self-worth, and meaning. If someone says they've not ever thought about God's existence, I'd argue they're lying to themselves. So, *does* God exist? There are three primary modes of thought the culture will use to answer this question: Atheism, Theism, and Pantheism. Atheism is the simple notion that God does not exist, and everything means nothing. Atheism parades itself as the absence of needing faith to exist, however I love the way Lee Strobel explained the reality of this worldview:

> *"To continue in atheism, I would need to believe that nothing produces everything, non-life produces life, randomness produces fine tuning, chaos produces information, unconsciousness produces consciousness, and non-reason produces reason. I simply don't have that much faith."*

The majority of people throughout history, however, have determined that there is, at the very least, a case for God's existence and this is what we call Theism. Theism can be interpreted one of two ways: Monotheism or polytheism. Monotheism is the belief that there is just one God, this would encompass the Christian, Jewish, and Muslim religions. Polytheism is the belief that there are multiple gods, and this would encompass religions such as Hinduism and Taoism. The third way that culture answers the question, *"Does God exist?"* is with the concept of pantheism, which means that everything that exists is God, this includes eastern religions such as Shintoism and Buddhism. There are multiple other ways to dissect these belief systems even further, but, for the sake of brevity, these simple breakdowns will be helpful for you and your nations to understand as they navigate their faith in a culture full of conflicting worldviews.

1. **Atheism** – God does not exist.

2. **Theism** – God does exist.

    a. **Monotheism** – there is one God.

    b. **Polytheism** – there are multiple gods.

3. **Pantheism** – Everything that exists is God.

While these three concepts answer the main question of whether or not God exists, there is a secondary question that must be asked if God does in fact exist and it is this, *"what is He like?"* This secondary question creates the sap of our theology that filters truth for our worldview; to know what God is like is to know his heart for His creation, including each one of us. While many religions have taken a shot at answering this secondary question over centuries of time, the only faith to be able to thoroughly give light to what God is like and how to have a relationship with Him is Christianity. Christianity makes the claim that God reveals Himself to us within creation and through the Bible. We are able to truly know God's character, qualities, and personality through the observation of the creation around us and by studying the Word that leads us to Him. Between thorough examination of these two things—creation and the word of God, an overwhelmingly substantial case has been made for the existence of God: Father, Son, and Holy Spirit.

I want to clarify that the goal of this section's content is not to give full scientific and physical proof that God is real, rather it is to reveal a strong case of evidence that will help you point your nations to the wonder of His existence. Each human has been given the road of reason to follow until it reaches the point of faith's necessity. At this crossroad (faith and reason) we each have the choice to put our faith in whatever we so choose, this is the essence of free will; whether we believe God exists or not will require faith. Although there is much evidence for the existence of God, at the end of the day there is never going to be a way to prove it with 100% certainty, for, as Dietrich Bonhoeffer once said, *"A God who let us prove his existence would be an idol."* God doesn't want a nation of robots who carry Him as a golden idol, rather a nation of sons and daughters who live in relationship with Him as a Father, and He promises that if we seek Him, we will find him (**Jeremiah 29:13**). Seeking isn't a passive act of convenience, it's a heart of pursuit that begins on the path of reason and ultimately flies by the wings of faith!

"A God who let us prove his existence would be an idol."
– Dietrich Bonhoeffer

God gives both general and special revelation to point towards His existence. General revelation is God all around us, it's the Apostle Paul's proclamation in **Romans 1:20,** "ALL THINGS PROCLAIM THE EXISTENCE OF GOD." We can teach our nations to go outside and look at the world around them: examine a leaf, feel the wind in their face, or watch the squirrels gather food as the cold sets in and understand God is caring, thoughtful, and creative. Special revelation, however, is how God intimately and specifically communicates with each one of us through the Bible, through Christ, and through direct connection with our hearts. We can direct our nations in special revelation by teaching them to study the word, pray, hear God's voice, and to know Jesus and the person of the Holy Spirit. In addition to general and special revelation, there is another way to discern the case for God's existence and that is by using our minds to make sense of what is taking place in and around us. There are many Christian theologians and philosophers over the centuries that have compiled and created logical arguments that shed light on the existence of God, of those are six primary arguments that I'd like to list and explain in this section. You can also search "proofs of God's existence" on YouTube and find many great videos to explain these concepts a little further. As you read through the following arguments, get familiar with them for yourself, and begin good conversations with your nations to create space for critical thinking. When they learn to think critically and pursue God diligently, our kids will become comfortable being able to not only share their faith but defend it when necessary.

SIX PROOFS OF GOD'S EXISTENCE

1. **Internal Witness** – This idea recognizes that we all have a sense deep inside of us that God exists. Paul refers to the unbeliever in **Romans 1:21,** "FOR EVEN THOUGH THEY KNEW GOD, THEY DID NOT HONOR HIM AS GOD OR GIVE THANKS, BUT THEY BECAME FUTILE IN THEIR REASONINGS, AND THEIR SENSELESS HEARTS WERE DARKENED." In verse 25 he goes on to say, "FOR THEY EXCHANGED THE TRUTH OF GOD FOR FALSEHOOD, AND WORSHIPED AND SERVED THE CREATURE RATHER THAN THE CREATOR…" The sense is that it's not just a believer who has a recognition of God deep inside, but all of creation is given this internal witness, what we do with that witness is up to us.

2. External Witness – God has not only placed the longing inside of us to search for Him, but He additionally reveals Himself externally through the wonder of creation so that we can find Him in all things. I love to work outside in my gardens, and I often see the existence of God through preparing the soil, planting seeds, watering, and watching fruit grow from seemingly nowhere; as I harvest the garden and feast on the abundance, it testifies of His masterful and detailed craftsmanship on the earth. "FOR SINCE THE CREATION OF THE WORLD HIS INVISIBLE ATTRIBUTES, THAT IS, HIS ETERNAL POWER AND DIVINE NATURE, HAVE BEEN CLEARLY PERCEIVED, BEING UNDERSTOOD BY WHAT HAS BEEN MADE, SO THAT THEY ARE WITHOUT EXCUSE." **- Romans 1:20**. Creation alone has given sufficient evidence that God is the Creator of it all!

"All things proclaim the existence of God."
*– **Napoleon Bonaparte***

3. Cosmological Argument – This argument explains that, scientifically, everything in the universe has a cause, therefore the universe itself must have a cause, and that cause is God. We can trace any object backwards to find the cause of its existence. Use my sweater for example: something caused the threads to be woven together to make the sweater, then something had to cause the cotton to be twisted into thread, then something caused the cotton to grow, etc. until we follow the cause all the way back to the beginning of the foundations of the earth, and then we must ask, *"what caused the universe?"* We believe the cause was God and He created it!

4. Teleological Argument – This is another way to explain intelligent design—the idea that everything has order and harmony, therefore it must have an intelligent Designer behind it. When we order a brand-new laptop it's common sense to know that the manufacturer didn't take a chunk of plastic, bits of glass, and a hundred microchips and throw them into a mixer, hope for the best, and randomly turn out a functional laptop. No, we understand that intricate objects like electronics are thoughtfully designed, crafted, and assembled. We look at the wonder of life in the same way; we cannot possibly explain the beautiful order and harmony of nature by simply saying a bunch of cells and genetic codes were thrown into a space together, shaken up, and randomly created a functional, intricate, and intuitive design.

5. Moral Standard – This argument deals with the conscience, which is our internal compass of right and wrong. The moral argument for God is founded upon the reality that moral law exists in the conscience of every human being. Whether or not we follow that moral compass is up to each one of us. Right and wrong isn't necessarily new, but we do culturally redefine what we want to place in the categories of right and wrong, so we must agree that there has to be a standard of good in order to rightly divide what is good and what is not. This is where the road leads to God as the standard of good. How do we know that it's morally wrong to set fire to a building full of people? How do we know that it is morally good to help an elderly person across the street? Even if it's explained as human nature, then our nature must be founded in something greater than ourselves that would establish the standard of good. God is the moral lawgiver and has crafted a moral compass within each and every human.

6. **Ontological Argument** – Okay, this last one is a real head scratcher. This argument is more of a conceptual truth and is well summed up by this statement,

"If it is possible that God exists, then it follows logically that God does exist." – Anselm.

In simple terms, the possibility of God existing in the natural world gives evidence that He, in fact, can and does. I know, it's a mind bender! For all of you who love a good philosophical thought process, I encourage you to visit Dr Craig videos on YouTube and search for "ontological argument" for more examination and explanation of this concept.

We can see that there is substantial evidence in creation, history, and revelation that points to the existence of God. Let's move to the secondary question, "What is God like?" More importantly, *can* we know what God is like? Jesus told His disciples, "WHOEVER HAS SEEN ME HAS SEEN THE FATHER." (**John 14:9**). The life of Jesus reveals the nature of God, and the scriptures thoroughly expound on the qualities of His likeness and character, so we need not look far for direction. In addition to scriptures, we can see God's qualities in nature, in relationships, and in His presence. As a young mom, I created a document that lists many of God's attributes with scripture references, and I would hang this paper around the house as the kids were growing up to remind them of who God is. I think we still have a water-spotted, wrinkled copy hanging on by a thread on our bathroom mirror. I've compiled a few attributes with the scripture references below. I encourage you to search the scriptures attached to each attribute, and let it permeate your soul as you discover more of Him. If you would like to download the entire document for free, so that you can hang it up in your home and use it as a tool to guide your nations in discovering who God is, visit the toolbox tab on our website.

WHO IS GOD?

He will never leave me or forsake me – **Hebrews 13:5**

He sets me free – **John 8:36**

He is my Shepherd – **Psalm 23:1**

He loves me – **1 John 4:11**

He healed me – **1 Peter 2:24**

He is my rock – **1 Corinthians 10:4**

He is the author and finisher – **Hebrews 12:2**

He is the creator of all things – **1 Peter 4:19**

He is my comforter – **John 14:16**

He is my rescuer and protector – **Psalm 91:14**

He is slow to anger and is compassionate – **Psalm 103:8**

He makes His ways known – **Psalm 103:7**

He can be found when you seek Him – **Jeremiah 29:13**

He has great plans for me – **Jeremiah 29:11**

He answers prayers – **Psalm 91:15**

He is Peace – **2 Thessalonians 3:16**

He is hope – **Romans 15:13**

He makes the impossible, possible – **Matthew 19:26**

He is the giver of good gifts – **Luke 11:13**

THE CASE FOR CHRIST

There are multiple religions that have come to the probable and intelligent conclusion that there is, in fact, a significant case for

God's existence, but there is one that stands unique to the rest, Christianity. Christianity is unique in the sense that our belief in Christ—His life, death and most importantly His resurrection—changes everything in the human experience. Christians believe that God finds value in and wants to have a personal relationship with each human being. The entire plan of creation, redemption, and restoration has been for the sole purpose of restoring the relationship between man and God. All throughout the Old Testament, God has made ways for redemption, yet each time His people would fall back into rebellion against Him. God then promises that He would visit His people and rescue them through a coming Messiah. Flip forward to the New Testament and we see that Jesus comes to proclaim the good news, as stated in Mark chapter 1, "THE TIME IS FULFILLED, AND THE KINGDOM OF HEAVEN IS AT HAND; REPENT AND BELIEVE THE GOSPEL." Jesus is the unique bridge between man and God; Jesus is God's reach for mankind, where all other religions require man to strive and reach for God. When we understand questions like, *"Who is Jesus?"*, *"Is He God?"*, *"How do we know?"* it truly changes everything.

"The scandal of the Christian religion is that God has completely revealed Himself to us through the historical life of Christ."

Who Is Jesus? The scriptures reveal that Jesus is the Son of God, who came to earth to seek and save the lost. Jesus is the Way, the Truth, and the Life, and leading your nations to the foot of the cross is of single and utmost importance to anything else you will teach them in this life. Along with scriptures, there are multiple Jewish and Roman sources such as Josephus and Tacitus that give much historical evidence describing the life and death of Christ. Let's first look at the scriptures to understand the beauty of who Jesus is:

WHO IS JESUS?

- He is the savior - **1 John 4:14**
- He is the way to the Father - **John 14:6**
- He is our brother - **Hebrews 2:11**
- He is our friend - **John 15:12-15**
- He is our redeemer - **Isaiah 47:4**
- He is our deliverer - **Psalm 34:17**
- He is our healer - **Acts 10:38**
- He is the Word - **John 1:14**
- He is God - **John 8:58**
- He was the first to be resurrected from the dead - **Colossians 1:18**
- He is Lord over all - **Acts 2:36**
- He cares for you - **1 Peter 5:7**
- He is alive! - **Romans 6:9**
- He suffered for you - **1 Peter 2:21**

scriptures are a revelational roadmap of Jesus' existence, and we know the word of God is reliable. It is helpful, however, to understand that there is another level of evidence for Christ's life, death, and resurrection in the historical world. Knowing how to have thoughtful conversations with unbelievers who don't believe that the Bible is a good source of proof is life-changing for our nations as they bring the gospel to the world.

IS JESUS GOD?

The resurrection is the crown jewel to the Christian faith, it is what makes Jesus God—for any man can live and die, but only One has risen again! I had a friend challenge me one Easter to wonder why we as Christians celebrate Christmas so extravagantly, yet we seem to swiftly brush over Easter with a single Sunday dedicated to a church service and brunch. *"We are, after all, resurrection people"*, he said, *"Of all holidays, we should really make a big deal out of this one!"* This hit my heart like an arrow many years ago. The birth of Christ is the most precious gift God could ever give, but it wasn't the extent of it, it was the seed of what was to come. The resurrection of Christ was the grand finale—the unwrapping of the promises of God and the ultimate transference of His inheritance to us! This mindset shift caused our family to start putting a bigger extravagance and meditation on resurrection season. We devote evenings to scripture, reflection, and hymns, we aim to go to church every day during Easter week, remembering each and every moment of the Friday-Sunday process, fasting and giving, and finally making a big deal on Easter Sunday to celebrate the wonder of what it means to be resurrection people! The resurrection is not only scriptural and spiritual, but also historical and able to be investigated. This is one of my favorite subjects to walk my teenagers through because it's the single most important piece of their faith, as the Apostle Paul exhorted: "FOR IF THE DEAD ARE NOT RAISED, NOT EVEN CHRIST HAS BEEN RAISED. AND IF CHRIST HAS NOT BEEN RAISED, YOUR FAITH IS FUTILE, AND YOU ARE STILL IN YOUR SINS. THEN THOSE ALSO WHO HAVE FALLEN ASLEEP IN CHRIST HAVE PERISHED. IF IN CHRIST WE HAVE HOPE IN THIS LIFE ONLY, WE ARE OF ALL PEOPLE MOST TO BE PITIED." – **1 CORINTHIANS 15:16-19**

THE ABCs OF THE RESURRECTION

In order to prove that the resurrection really happened, three things would need to be true: Jesus had to live, He had to die, and then He had to live again. Scripture clearly states the facts of all three of these events, and there are multiple historical sources that corroborate the evidence. As Christians, we live by faith and not by scientific proof, so I am in no way suggesting that our faith in Christ rests upon the proof of man's evidence and wisdom, however it is a beautiful thing when reason and faith are able to support one another to give evidence that points to truth and leaves man without excuse. Here is a quick overview of the "ABCs" that validate the resurrection:

A. **Jesus had to live** – In order to validate the assertion of any historical event, the "rule of 3" is most often applied, which means you need three independent sources to corroborate a claim. Bryan Windle states at least 10 ancient sources that document Jesus' life and crucifixion[12], which is more than enough historical proof. In addition to this, the scriptures are clear, "FOR I DELIVERED TO YOU AS OF FIRST IMPORTANCE WHAT I ALSO RECEIVED: THAT CHRIST DIED FOR OUR SINS IN ACCORDANCE WITH THE SCRIPTURES, THAT HE WAS BURIED, THAT HE WAS RAISED ON THE THIRD DAY IN ACCORDANCE WITH THE SCRIPTURES" – **1 CORINTHIANS 15:3-4**

B. **Jesus had to die** – As stated above, there is overwhelming historical proof of Christ's life and death. In fact, so many scholars, both Christian and non-Christian, consider it an indisputable fact that Jesus was crucified that you'd be labeled a lunatic if you tried to say otherwise!

C. **Jesus had to live again** – As the Apostle Paul has mentioned, the most important event that the Christian faith hinges on is the resurrection of Christ: without the resurrection, our faith is useless. The Holy Spirit is the greatest individual proof we have of Christ being alive, as we interact with His Spirit and come to know Him personally, we recognize the validity of a risen King. In addition to the personal witness of the Spirit, it's impressive historical proof that more than 500 people, individuals and groups, at one time reported to have seen Jesus after His resurrection. The

Apostle Paul reported, "AND THAT HE APPEARED TO CEPHAS, THEN TO THE TWELVE. THEN HE APPEARED TO MORE THAN FIVE HUNDRED BROTHERS AT ONE TIME, MOST OF WHOM ARE STILL ALIVE, THOUGH SOME HAVE FALLEN ASLEEP. THEN HE APPEARED TO JAMES, THEN TO ALL THE APOSTLES. LAST OF ALL, AS TO ONE UNTIMELY BORN, HE APPEARED ALSO TO ME." – **1 CORINTHIANS 15:5-8**

WHO IS THIS HOLY SPIRIT?

The Holy Spirit, though we are mentioning Him last, is certainly not least, in fact, He is the greatest advantage we have in living out our faith every day. He is often considered the forgotten member of the trinity because He is overlooked and misunderstood. When the disciples were filled with sorrow upon hearing of Jesus' imminent departure, He assured them,

> "BUT I TELL YOU THE TRUTH, IT IS TO YOUR ADVANTAGE THAT I GO AWAY; FOR IF I DO NOT GO AWAY, THE HELPER (COMFORTER, ADVOCATE, INTERCESSOR—COUNSELOR, STRENGTHENER, STANDBY) WILL NOT COME TO YOU; BUT IF I GO, I WILL SEND HIM (THE HOLY SPIRIT) TO YOU [TO BE IN CLOSE FELLOWSHIP WITH YOU]." –**JOHN 16:7 (AMP)**

Jesus knew what the disciples didn't grasp at the time: that the Holy Spirit would bring the believers together and be their advantage, their benefit, their edge over the competition of the enemy. The Holy Spirit is the checkmate to the devil and the key to a successful life in Christ. Second to salvation, the Holy Spirit is the most important treasure you will lead your nations to discover. I exhort you, don't overlook Him! Let's look at a few scriptures to draw out the gold of the Holy Spirit:

WHO IS THE HOLY SPIRIT?

- He's called God - **Acts 5:3-4**
- He's called the Spirit of God - **Genesis 1:2**
- He's treated as equal to God the Father and Son - **Matthew 3:16**
- He's eternal - **Hebrews 9:14**
- He's sovereign - **Zechariah 12:10**
- He was involved with creation - **Genesis 1:1–2**
- He enabled the writing of the Bible - **2 Peter 1:21**
- He helps us to recognize the glory of God - **2 Corinthians 4:4**
- He enables us to call upon Jesus as Lord - **1 Corinthians 12:13**
- He teaches us all things - **John 14:26**
- He helps us remember what we've learned - **John 14:26**
- He leads us and guides us into all truth - **John 16:13**
- He helps us pray - **Romans 8:26-27**
- He convicts unbelievers of sin - **John 16:8-9**
- He convicts believers of righteousness - **John 16:8,10**
- He convicts Satan of his own condemnation - **John 16:8,11**
- He gives us gifts of the Spirit - **1 Corinthians 12:11**
- He empowers us for ministry and life - **Acts 1:8**

The Holy Spirit is a person, and your nations can know Him just as they know the Father and Jesus. Let's teach our nations that being filled with the Spirit is a normal part of the Christian experience and is an integral part of a victorious life of discipleship. Aristotle once said, *"Matter seems to fill up whatever space it's been given"*, and, in the same way, the Holy Spirit will continue to fill up whatever space He is invited into. There are several ways that we can encourage our nations to be filled and continue being filled with the Holy Spirit, here are a few listed in scripture:

BEING FILLED WITH THE HOLY SPIRIT

1. We are filled by faith – **Galatians 3:14**
2. We are filled through baptism, both water and Spirit – **Acts 2:38, Acts 19:1-6**
3. We are filled by obedience – **Acts 5:32**
4. We are filled before we believe – **John 3:5**
5. We are continually filled after we believe – **Ephesians 5:18**

KNOWING THE ONE

Listen, as a parent you will meet a myriad of problems to solve, lessons to teach, decisions to make, questions to answer, and issues to counsel. More often than not, you will come to acknowledge and accept that you don't have all the answers to the situations in life, but the great news is you know the One who does! I realize that these last couple of chapters feel very dense with information, but I am praying that there are nuggets in them that will help you navigate the journey of preparing your nations to shape their worldview and lock arms with their Creator. It's important that we help our children understand that they will never know it all, but they can know the One who holds it all, and by Him they can succeed in it all.

Extra Theology Resources:

- *"Defeating Darwinism"* by Phillip E. Johnson (9th-12th grade)
- *"Seeking Allah, Finding Jesus"* by Nabeel Qureshi
- *"A Case for Christ"* by Lee Strobel
- https://www.youtube.com/user/drcraigvideos - Reasonable Faith short video series

PRAYER

God, it's impossible to explain the gratitude that we hold in our hearts for who You are! We could search a thousand years and find none like You. We could write books for all eternity and still not fully capture the weight of your greatness. Would you reveal Yourself in a deeper way to our hearts each day? Would you peel the scales from my eyes and the eyes of my children to see You to the extent we are able, even with our human limitations? To know You is to know peace! To know You is to know the fullness of joy and pleasures abounding! To know You is to know the One who holds it all and causes success and progress in life! Empower me, Father, by Your Spirit to impart knowledge and a love for You to my children. Empower me with grace to be an example of pursuing You with my whole heart and my whole mind. Thank you for giving my children a love for Your word, Your truth, and Your presence. In Jesus name, AMEN!

REFLECTION/DISCUSSION QUESTIONS:

1. Where do I need to draw closer to know God? Father, Jesus, Holy Spirit?

2. What is one thing I can do to lead my children closer to Jesus?

3. How can I begin encouraging them to be filled with the Spirit in their current season of life? (look at the 5 ways to be filled with the Spirit)

CHAPTER 12

ORIGINAL DESIGN

"There is a design and a purpose for each of our lives.
Living unaware of that is sad, but dying unaware
of it is a tragedy." – **Lou Engle**

Every human life is framed with a unique function, we call this an "original design". Design refers to the blueprint or plan that was laid out for each individual, and the term "original" is defined as one being planned from the beginning. Therefore, we understand that God's original design for mankind was an intentional blueprint crafted before the earth was even formed. Paul reminds the church of this in **Ephesians 1:4-5,** "JUST AS HE CHOSE US IN HIM BEFORE THE FOUNDATION OF THE WORLD, THAT WE WOULD BE HOLY AND BLAMELESS BEFORE HIM. IN LOVE HE PREDESTINED US TO ADOPTION AS SONS THROUGH JESUS CHRIST TO HIMSELF, ACCORDING TO THE GOOD PLEASURE OF HIS WILL." The intention of God is that mankind would bear His image and carry a unique function of the Spirit in this life. The purpose for this would be to have a personal relationship with Him, and union with one another in the body of Christ.

There is no such thing as a DIY faith; we were never meant to do this thing called life and discipleship on our own. Certainly, we are individually called by God, to God, and for God, but we are corporately purposed to learn, grow, and mature in discipleship together within the body of believers. The Body of Christ is the holy nation that our children belong to, and, as we help them discover their individual design, we must also help them understand how they contribute to the Body as a whole.

> "So, in Christ we, though many, form one body, and each member belongs to all the others." – **Romans 12:5**

Remember at the beginning of this section when I gave the example of a worldview being about understanding the bigger picture of a puzzle? Well, original design is about our nations each having a unique piece to that puzzle; a core function which belongs to the overall plan of God. The unity of Spirit that we share as a Body of believers is the act of gathering under the banner of Jesus Christ and bringing our gifts and perspectives together to create the whole puzzle. When just one piece is missing the picture isn't complete—we need one another! We understand that we were created as a three-part man: spirit, soul, and body. We also understand from scripture that our original design—or individual function—can be broken down into three sub-parts as well: calling, purpose, and assignments.

> Now the word of the Lord came to me saying, 'before I formed you in the womb I knew you, and before you were born, I consecrated you; I have appointed you a prophet to the nations... See, I have appointed you this day over the nations and over the kingdoms, to pluck up and to break down, to destroy and to overthrow, to build and to plant." – **Jeremiah 1:4-5,10**

In this scripture, Jeremiah beautifully breaks down what the Lord has spoken to him about the three-fold function of man's original design: Calling, purpose and assignments. *Consecration, prophet, and nations* are the words that lay out the function of Jeremiah's life; God is showing him his original design through these three operations: the calling of consecration, the purpose of his gift as a prophet, and the assigned location and works that He is inviting Jeremiah to step into in each season. We've spent some time in this book discussing the larger picture that our nations belong to, and now we want to help these nations understand the original design of their unique and individual contribution to the larger picture. Understanding their original design can open up a world of opportunities for our nations to offer their piece to the puzzle in partnership with God and the Body of Christ. Together with God they will do great exploits!!

CALLING - UNIVERSAL

"BEFORE I FORMED YOU IN THE WOMB I KNEW YOU,
AND BEFORE YOU WERE BORN, I CONSECRATED YOU"

The first, foremost, and supreme function of our nations' original design is their calling. The calling of God is universal to every man, woman, and child, and that calling is Him. Simply put, our fundamental calling is to know and be known by God. Often times we use the word "calling" in regard to the gifts we hold, the roles we steward, or the works we are tasked with in life, such as being called to parenthood, being called to lead worship, or being called to move to another state. However, scripture reveals with much conviction that our calling is singular, and it is relationship with Him. "GOD IS FAITHFUL, WHO HAS CALLED YOU INTO FELLOWSHIP WITH HIS SON,

JESUS CHRIST OUR LORD" 1 Corinthians 1:9. God has given us a universal heavenly calling to share together as a body of believers (**Hebrews 3:1**) and it is our basis of being unified in the Spirit. God spoke to Jeremiah and said, *"I consecrated you..."* which signified that He had rooted Jeremiah's design in the source of honor, dedication, and sacred devotion to God first and foremost. This calling of consecration and holiness is encrypted in our children's design before they are even born. "EVEN AS HE CHOSE US IN HIM BEFORE THE FOUNDATION OF THE WORLD, THAT WE SHOULD BE HOLY AND BLAMELESS BEFORE HIM..." – **Ephesians 1:4**. Our calling is so fundamental that we cannot properly understand the purpose of our individual gifts or the assignments that God wants us to walk in if we do not first discover our anchor in the roots of our calling in Him. His nearness is our good. There is nothing on earth that will satisfy our nations' desires besides Him. To know Him and be known by Him; to love Him and be loved by Him, there is no higher call in this life.

EXCELSIOR!

Excelsior is a Latin adjective that means *ever upward!* Marvel creator, Stan Lee, has been credited with signing off his comic columns with the phrase, "Excelsior!" and in 2010 he tweeted his personal interpretation, *"Upward and onward to greater glory!"* We can find inspiration as believers in Stan Lee's interpretation because God has truly called us ever upward to His greater glory!

"I PRESS ON TOWARD THE GOAL FOR THE PRIZE OF THE UPWARD CALL OF GOD IN CHRIST JESUS." – **PHILIPPIANS 3:14**

The upward calling on our nations' lives is the source and production of these three things: identity in Christ, confidence through Christ, and surrender to Christ. We live in a culture of people that passionately seek for identity in sexual orientation, confidence in personal accomplishment, while surrendering to the pursuit of pleasure and pious ideals, yet we've never been more mentally depraved and spiritually dry. It's as if after thousands of years on earth, the human condition still understands the absolute need for identity, confidence, and surrender, but continues to come up empty when seeking the world for help finding it.

A core fruit of our calling in Christ is that it defines and roots our spiritual <u>identity in Him</u>. The first time I spoke publicly was at a women's conference back in 2011, there were eight of us invited to share for 10-minutes on a topic of our choice, and I chose to share on identity. I spoke on this topic because it was one of the first messages God had used to rewire my soul; I knew myself geographically—living on earth, but I had not yet understood who I was positionally—seated in Heaven. Now when the word "identity" is uttered today, it often comes with the implication of knowing who *I am*. However, when God took me through this journey of identity so many years ago, it was first and centrally focused on who *He is*. After spending many months discovering a right understanding of who God is, He then began to show me who I am *in* Him. To rightly know who He is, is to rightly know who you are. As foundational as it is for us as Christians to understand our identity, I fear that we have created golden calves out of who we are at the expense of not fully beholding who He is. Identity is not so much about the attributes of who we are, but who we belong to. This is where our confidence comes from, not of ourselves, but of the One we are tethered to. We must become like the Apostle Paul in **2 Corinthians 3** "Such confidence we have toward God through Christ. Not that we are adequate in ourselves so as to consider anything as having come from ourselves, but our adequacy is from God." For further discovery of who God is, consider downloading the "Who He Is" document from our website listed under the resources section at the end of this chapter.

Just as described in 2 Corinthians 3, our calling also produces confidence through Christ. Before I understood my calling in Christ, I would cart around my insecurities, seeking for some semblance of confidence; there were two ways I would walk into a room: with arrogance or false humility, both of which are rooted in pride. I would either arrogantly find a way to be better than anyone in the room—more charismatic, funny, interesting, and smart—or I would falsely humble myself and decide that I stunk and wasn't as good as anyone in that room, then I would self-hate, self-reject, and self-sabotage. As God walked me through the understanding of my calling, I began to realize that authentic confidence through Christ is seeing that, because He did a thorough, finished work on the cross, in Him we are all equal in value, each bearing uniqueness to celebrate, and are now co-laborers with the magnificent plan that is unfolding. Training our nations to find their confidence rooted in their calling to Christ will open a world of freedom for them to contribute to the overall plan of God instead of competing for attention from others. This creates opportunities for them to edify and empower others without being fearful that it will take away from the confidence they have through Christ!

Finally, our calling produces freedom through surrender to God. Our calling is spiritually and vertically focused, yet, physically, we live in the tension of a horizontally centered existence, and these two directions seem to ever be at odds with one another. We've never been a busier, more stressed out, overwhelmed society of humans than we are today. There are a multitude of problems to solve, decisions to make, people to reach, tasks to complete, and needs to meet. It's incredibly easy to wake up with those things clawing for real estate in our thoughts and emotions daily. This is why it's so important to teach our nations that surrender to God is the strength to their purpose and the success of their assignments. When we understand that we were designed for Him, and His nearness is our good, then we stop fussing about the horizontal demands of life and rest in the vertical power of His presence, receiving His provision for our needs. He promises that if we seek first the kingdom that He will add all things to us (**Matthew 6:33**). If we lean on Him, He will make the crooked places straight (**Proverbs 3:5-6**). If we give Him the right to direct our lives, He will pull it off perfectly (**Psalm 37:5**). If **Isaiah 54:13** exhorts that my children are taught of the *Lord* and great is their peace, then why do I need to fuss about their issues? Why wouldn't I surrender it to the Lord and let Him do what He does best? He's good at what He does, trust me, I've tried it both ways, and I can tell you that God can get infinitely more done with our prayers than He can with our stressed-out striving works. Having teen and young adult nations in our home has caused conversations of surrender to come up more often now than it did when they were little, because they too, are starting to understand the pull of life's issues, so I have been spending much time these days reinforcing, redirecting, and encouraging the journey of surrender to God.

Surrendering to Christ can take shape in many ways, whether through quiet time, redirecting thoughts throughout the day, or verbally worshiping Him in the midst of challenges. I personally start each morning by receiving His grace for the day, fixing my eyes on Him, and verbally calling out His attributes in worship. I start most of my days with confessing and declaring the word of God over myself, my family, and my home to set the tone of truth in my mind and heart. Surrendering to Him is a fruit of beholding who He is; if you know Him, you'd want nothing more than to surrender to Him, He's just that good!

PURPOSE - INDIVIDUAL

"I HAVE APPOINTED YOU A PROPHET TO THE NATIONS."

The second function of mankind's original design is his individual purpose. Your nations' purpose is secondary to their calling, and it is the unique and individual part they play in God's overall plan for redemption. Each human being has been wired with a purposeful set of gifts and tools to use for the betterment of life and the advancement of the kingdom. I interpret individual purpose as a two-fold function: <u>motivational</u> and <u>missional</u>. Motivation is about what moves us into action, are you motivated by practical needs to be filled? Are you moved by someone who needs encouragement? Is it a problem that needs to be solved? God told Jeremiah that he had been appointed as a prophet to the nations, which signified that his purpose was to speak encouragement, warning, and insights to the people for God; Jeremiah's primary purpose in life was to function as a prophet. Scripture lays out more ways to discover our purpose through the Grace Gifts of Romans 12, and, since I've already written on it, I'll just encourage you to flip back to chapter nine for a refresher. Whatever your nation's motivation, it is what propels them into the second part of their purpose, which is their personal mission. Their mission is their "why", the goal of their action. *Why do I want to encourage others? Why do I want to show compassion? Why do I want to fill this need?* For example, if your nation has a motivation of service—to fill practical needs, they may discover that their mission in filling those needs is to bring things into order. Another example might be that your nation is motivated by encouraging others to overcome adversity and keep pressing on—exhortation, and his reason or mission for encouraging is to see people fulfill their destiny.

"THROUGH OUR UNION WITH CHRIST WE TOO HAVE BEEN CLAIMED BY GOD AS HIS OWN INHERITANCE. BEFORE WE WERE EVEN BORN, HE GAVE US OUR DESTINY, THAT WE WOULD FULFILL THE PLAN OF GOD WHO ALWAYS ACCOMPLISHES EVERY PURPOSE AND PLAN IN HIS HEART." **- EPHESIANS 1:11**

Paul explains in **Romans 12:6** that we each have "GIFTS DIF-
FERING ACCORDING TO THE GRACE THAT WAS GIVEN TO US", so we
understand that a measure of grace is necessary for each of us to
operate in the gifts given to us by God. Without grace we end up
frustrated and striving. Grace is all sufficiency and power in our
weakness so that no man may boast, *"look what I've done!"* This is
great news for our nations because we can encourage them not to
focus on all that they cannot do, but to trust God to use them powerfully in spite of it. There is so much power in knowing that "GOD
IS ABLE TO MAKE ALL GRACE OVERFLOW TO YOU, SO THAT, ALWAYS HAV-
ING ALL SUFFICIENCY IN EVERYTHING, YOU MAY HAVE AN ABUNDANCE
FOR EVERY GOOD DEED" **2 Corinthians 9:8**. Why would we want
to do life any other way?! One of the ways we encourage our children to find where God has placed grace and power in their gifts
is to examine where they feel their greatest struggle is; wherever
you find a prominent weakness is usually where God will use His
grace most powerfully! For example, my daughter, Evelyn, tends
to wrestle with anxiety and oppressive thoughts, but as God has
rooted her in her calling and has revealed her purpose, He gives her
His grace to overcome mental adversity and then use her gifts to
exhort and release prophetic encouragement to others. I have similar challenges and gifts as Evelyn, and I used to feel like it was an
impossible ask for God to put me in a position to pray for and counsel others through mental dysfunction while I myself was working
to overcome. I would soon realize that **Proverbs 11:25** says this
is precisely how we are *going* to overcome – "...AND HE WHO WATERS
WILL ALSO HIMSELF BE WATERED." In your greatest struggle, you will
likely find your greatest purpose!

For further discovery of your nation's individual purpose, consider having them take the Grace Gifts test and read through the
Grace Gifts documents in the toolbox tab of our website, which is
listed under the resources section at the end of this chapter.

ASSIGNMENTS - SEASONAL

"SEE, I HAVE APPOINTED YOU THIS DAY OVER THE
NATIONS... TO PLUCK UP AND TO BREAK DOWN, TO
DESTROY AND TO OVERTHROW, TO BUILD AND TO PLANT."

The third function of our original design that we are exploring is our assignments. Our assignments come last in the grand scheme of things, not because they matter the least of all the three parts of our function, but because they have the greatest dependency on our calling and purpose. Without the roots of our calling, we cannot understand our purpose, and without calling and purpose, we will burnout in our assignments. Assignments must be approached *from* our identity not *for* an identity.

"WE ARE HIS WORKMANSHIP, CREATED IN CHRIST JESUS FOR GOOD
WORKS, WHICH GOD PREPARED BEFOREHAND SO THAT WE WOULD
WALK IN THEM." – **EPHESIANS 2:10**

Our assignments are seasonal, they are the good works that God has called us to right here and now: problems to solve, decisions to make, roles to steward, and impact to bring, and they tend to change with the times and seasons that pass. Assignments can pertain to family life, career, ministry, personal development, and relationship with the Lord. The Apostle Paul spoke of these good works in his letter to the Ephesians as plural in nature because we were not designed to function in one single assignment throughout our entire life. The culture, spiritual climate, and social systems continue to change, thus causing the needs around us to change, therefore God invites us to tackle assignments according to what is needed in each season. There are seasons when my assignment is solely focused on my household and homeschooling my children, then there are other seasons that I've stepped into various roles such as writing, speaking, going to school, counseling, teaching, podcasting, etc. To fully understand what your assignments are in each season, it's imperative for you to keep a dialogue with the Lord as things shift and move with time. When we teach our nations to lean into their assignments and stay in their lane, it will cause their hearts to be focused, peaceful, and prosperous no matter the chaos that may be breaking out around them. Every good thing begins in prayer, so teach your children to pray continually about the issues their heart is being pulled to solve. Ask God to give them wisdom and discernment on how to utilize what they have in their hand to walk in the assignment He has for them in their current season. Remember that the "how will I do this" of our assignments is found in the "who am I becoming." We are verbs, not nouns, and God continues to mature us as disciples to function in our assignments. He will unlock new talents, discoveries, and resources in your nations as He brings them to the good works that He has for them. Don't get stuck in trying to figure out how to make it work. Instead, teach them to pray and ask God who He's helping them become in order to accomplish their mission—the resources will follow!

DISCERNING TIMES AND SEASONS

> "There is a time and season for every activity under the heavens." — Ecclesiastes 3:1

If you're anything like me, one of the first things I check with my morning coffee is the weather app—I find it helpful to know whether I should put on a swimsuit or a snowsuit. We live in Minnesota, and it is a well-known fact that the weather around here can change so dramatically that we've often experienced multiple seasons in the span of just two short hours. One minute you're outside enjoying the hot sun and the next minute a cold wind is picking up and it starts to snow. Just as we can look to the sky and see the weather changing and then prepare to respond in the physical realm, we can also look to the spiritual and cultural climates and discern seasons of what God is doing. Our culture and society are ever changing and always evolving from generation to generation, we cannot stop it. Even the recent pandemic has ushered in a significant shift of culture, and it's apparent that it's not going back. If we want our nations to be effective ambassadors of the kingdom, we must teach them to stay meek and pliable to what God is doing in each season of life. If you think you know all there is to know about the world, and you spend your time trying to avoid the current realities or forcing the society around you into an ideal of "what should be", you will never capture or thrive in what God is doing right now. Assignments are the wonderful partnership we have with God's plans, therefore how we stay connected to Him, and how we show up for each season will be the deciding factor of success. A few practical ways you can engage with your own assignments, and help your nations do the same, are to ask, observe, and understand.

ASK: Ask God what He's up to in the current season, and then ask Him to show you how He wants you to partner with Him. Ask God to give you a vision to see the assignments that are relevant to you right now.

OBSERVE: What are the main issues that seem to be popping up often? There are times when I notice things like multiple people dealing with mental health crises, physical sickness, or marriage issues/divorce. Listen for words and phrases that keep coming up, "identity", "revival", "alignment", etc. When you observe a pattern of issues or themes around you then seek to understand...

UNDERSTAND: As you observe and identify what is happening around you, begin to seek for who God is in it: *Healer, Provider, Father...* Knowing God's nature from scripture and personal experience will help you identify who He is through it all. When you study the scriptures and experience Him as the God of restoration, revival, healing, increase, suffering, etc. then you'll easily identify Him in the midst of the season's victories and challenges. Secondarily, it will be helpful to understand how you will need to grow in order to accomplish the assignment that He is inviting you into. When God invited me into the assignment of book writing I had no experience with publishing, marketing, or even formal writing, I had to learn and grow in these areas, which included getting connected with the right people to help me accomplish the task. Here are a few more questions to help discern your assignments in each season:

1. **Ask God what He is doing in this season, and ask Him how He wants you to partner with Him?**

2. **What issues or people groups is my heart drawn to?** (women/men/children, poverty, trafficking, equipping people, caring for sick, feeding the hungry, political systems, legal function etc.)

3. **What does God show you about these issues? Which ones are for you and which ones are not?** (We are not called to tackle everything we see, even if we want to.)

4. What roles of responsibility do I have right now? (career, family, hobbies, charity etc.) **Is there anything I am still trying to do that is no longer "in season" for me?**

5. Who am I becoming in order to function in my current assignment? (a pioneer, a prayer warrior, increased in faith, student of the scriptures, clear communicator.)

God calls our nations to Himself, equips them with purpose in Him and creates good works for them to walk in with Him. What a beautiful design it is that we can each bring our unique part to the Body of Christ, sharpen each other, encourage each other, and celebrate each other. Together with God we will do great exploits!

Resources:

- *"The Essential Tozer Collection"* – the pursuit of God, the purpose of man, the crucified life, by A.W. Tozer
- *"Driven by Eternity"* by John Bevere
- www.occupy-freedom.com (Toobox > Grace Gifts)

CHAPTER 13

INTO ALL THE WORLD

"I alone cannot change the world, but I can cast a stone across the waters to create many ripples." – **Mother Teresa**

Pulling up to the tech school parking lot I could tell that my son was nervous to go in. We were a couple of minutes behind schedule to the culinary program orientation and there's only one thing that stretches Matthew more than acclimating to a new crowd of people—that is being late. I kept the mood light as we speed-walked through the double doors and searched the empty hallways for signs to tell us the right direction. In pursuit of a crowd of white chef's coats, I noticed multiple items hanging on the walls of the auditorium that told the story of an especially diverse audience attending this school. *"Lord, help me see what You're up to"* I prayed under my breath. I remembered how we had dropped off our daughter, Evelyn, just a couple of years before at a private Christian university. I remembered how peaceful the campus felt and how the praises of God spilled from the mouths of every professor, with banners hanging high in the corridors, littered with scripture. This experience felt immensely different. We found the event room and tip-toed our way through the standing chefs who were introducing themselves and found a seat alongside the rest of the aspiring culinary professionals. I looked around and became aware of the motley crew of personalities, faith, ages, experiences, and social stances represented in one single room. My heart tightened a bit as I thought about all of the years of dedicated homeschooling and intentional training that we had invested into our son, and now he was going to sit among an intensely different culture of influence every day for the next two years. In the midst of questioning whether we'd made a mistake choosing this school and this program, God broke through. *"The fire is going to awaken the Word within him"*, I heard the Holy Spirit say to me, *"Don't be afraid, trust Me, and trust what you've poured into him for the past 17 years!"* It was then that I knew the Lord was up to something good, as He prepared my nations to go into all the world.

THE GREAT ASSIGNMENT

Remember at the beginning of this section we have talked about how a worldview is two-parts: our view *of* the world and our view *for* the world. We've spent much time so far looking through the first lens, so let's talk mission. This second part of our worldview is missional; your view *for* the world. Being "missional" describes the perspective to see people as God does and to engage in the activity of reaching them.[13] Jesus exhorted us in Luke,

> "AND THE MASTER SAID TO THE SLAVE, 'GO OUT INTO THE ROADS AND THE HEDGES AND PRESS UPON THEM TO COME IN, SO THAT MY HOUSE WILL BE FILLED." – **LUKE 14:23**

The greatest assignment of our nations' lives is that they would go into all the world and share Christ: the hope of glory that is in them (**Colossians 1:27**). The only reason we would spend an entire section of this book gaining understanding of how to shape our nations' view of and for the world is so that they can use what is in them to partner with God's plan and be a source of restoration to others.

I have noticed seasons with each of my children when they seem to stop growing in their hunger for God and start getting anxious, irritable, and all-consumed with worldly burdens, it's like an invisible threshold that signals it's time to start putting fire to the word that has been sown into them. Each time this signal comes up we start having conversations about how they can begin to give away what's inside of them so that they can get out of the swamp and get into the river, thus becoming a part of the advancement of the kingdom. At this point of tension, we start training them further in prayer, prophecy, and studying to share the message of the word with others. It's easy to get so caught up in pouring into our kids that we forget to teach them how to pour back out, this is the "in and out" mentality that Jesus spoke of in **John 10:9**, "I AM THE DOOR. IF ANYONE ENTERS BY ME, HE WILL BE SAVED AND WILL GO <u>IN AND OUT</u> AND FIND PASTURE." The key to abundant life and healthy discipleship is to go in and out and find pasture: to be in seasons of receiving and seasons of pouring out. Some of the environments of pouring out will be scary for us to send our nations into, and we must do so with wisdom by the Spirit, but it is imperative to their growth and strength that you allow them to be proofed by the fire and permit the word in them to be tested so that what is real can be reinforced and what is religion can be burnt out.

Our nations have such a light inside of them; they have gifts, talents, and keys to unlock the bondage of the oppressed. They are an answer to someone's prayers and this part of the journey is to prepare them to share it with the world. There is no greater assignment than that of sharing Jesus with those we come in contact with, and that means teaching our kids to share the hope that they have in every environment they find themselves in. The kingdom of heaven is at hand to heal, deliver, restore, and bring salvation and our nations are rising to take the baton of faith and go forth in the power of the Holy Spirit. It does us no good to spend years shaping our child's perspective and interpretation *of* the world if we have no intention of helping them become missional *for* the world with the hope of the kingdom!

Some practical insights to prepare your nations to go into the world…

Encourage Mentorship: Encourage your older teens to find a mentor. Someone who is a few seasons ahead of them and showing fruit in the areas of life that they want to be successful in—faith, marriage, family, career, etc. Remember this, a great start doesn't equal a great finish, so training them to seek wisdom from others and remain pliable to correction, encouragement, and mentorship is of lifelong value to their continued growth. As they grow into young adults, encourage them to begin mentoring someone younger than they are, so that they learn to utilize what God teaches them for the benefit of the whole and not just for their personal consumption. Mentoring a younger generation will also teach them to stay humble and learn from generations coming after them so they don't become crusty and set in the ways they see and experience life.

Grow in Discernment: Discernment means to judge well, especially to judge things that are particularly obscure and not blatantly obvious to divide. Discernment helps us walk upright in a world that offers us a multitude of doors to walk through, many of which seem to counterfeit another, like the wheat and tare. The bible names three ways that we can grow in discernment: Pray for wisdom (**James 1:5**), read the word to rightly divide truth so as to be able to identify clear counterfeits (**2 Timothy 2:15**), and practice using discernment in daily life (**Hebrews 5:14**). Therefore, pray for your nations to be discerning. Teach them to be strong in the word and then have meaningful dialogue with them about everyday life situations, challenging them to look beyond the superficial and discern the reality of the matter.

Be Strong in the Word: The word holds life. The word bears witness to truth. The word rightly divides. The word reveals God's character. The word is the sword of the Spirit that overcomes the enemy. Determine to be a steady example of living strong in the word, and then emphasize your nation's need to be strong in the word as well. This is an area I am working to do better in to be honest. I've read and studied my bible openly for twenty years, I've achieved a bachelor's in theology, I paste scriptures around the house, and I speak the word openly—whether through spiritual warfare or declaring truth and goodness over my household. I've led by example and my kids know full well that I discipline myself in the word, but I see now that I have relied too heavily on my example of discipleship as if they would catch their strength in the word like they catch a cold. We've had to adjust and have been working more these days to get into the word, teaching them to actively use it and love it because it truly is life, and without the word, this world doesn't make any sense. Our example alone isn't enough to train our nations in the word, let's follow it up by taking time to teach them more sufficiently to do it for themselves and to become lovers of the word. If you're feeling this lack in your training as well, it's never too late to start!

Create Confession Culture: Oh, so many hours we spend training, teaching, and empowering our children in the ways that God has purposed them and is sending them into the world! One thing we must not forget in those hours of spiritual training is to remind our nations of their humanity. To remind them that as much as they are spiritual and created for another world, they are also human with human experiences, and they need Jesus. We all do.

> "I WILL NOT SPEAK WITH YOU MUCH LONGER, FOR THE RULER OF
> THE WORLD (SATAN) IS COMING. AND HE HAS NO CLAIM ON ME [NO
> POWER OVER ME NOR ANYTHING THAT HE CAN USE AGAINST ME]"
> **–JOHN 14:30**

Remember when Jesus warned Peter that he was going to deny Him before the rooster crowed and Peter was like, *Nah, that's never happening, I'll go with you to the death!* Remember how Peter did actually deny Jesus three times? I wonder what would have come of Peter if he would have been able to believe about himself what Jesus already knew. So far as we are able to stand in our spiritual position as children of God, we must also be able to embrace our humanity and come to realize what God already knows about us; He knows our potential for shortcomings. Practicing and teaching a lifestyle of confession and repentance to our nations will keep them from being bogged down with the hidden pain of the human experience. When we say yes to Jesus, we become the righteousness of God in Christ, and we no longer identify with or practice sin. However, it's inevitable that temptation will knock and, whether in thought, attitude, or behavior, sometimes we will open that door. When this happens, we want our response to be running *to* God, not away from Him, and the way we practice this is by swift confession and repentance. Temptation is not a sin, every person is tempted, it's what you do with it that matters. Confessing to God what He already knows builds trust and intimacy, and confessing to our brothers and sisters builds vulnerability and connection. There is no shame in shortcomings, shame only takes hold when we let it convince us to hide our shortcomings. If we don't teach our nations that they will have failure, then how will they see a need for the Savior? And if we don't teach them that failure is a part of the human experience, how will they know that they can run *to* God for grace, instead of *away* from Him?

Teaching our nations to embrace their humanity and understand their need for the Savior and for the body of believers is their lifeline to a lifestyle of freedom.

"You can't stop a bird from landing on your head,
*but you can stop it from building a nest." – **Bill Johnson***

Be Full of the Spirit: Jesus revealed to His disciples, "BUT I TELL YOU THE TRUTH, IT IS TO YOUR ADVANTAGE THAT I GO AWAY; FOR IF I DO NOT GO AWAY, THE HELPER WILL NOT COME TO YOU; BUT IF I GO, I WILL SEND HIM TO YOU." – JOHN 16:7 The Holy Spirit is our advantage here on earth, He is the seal of promise of what is to come, He is our access to heaven on earth, and to live life without being full of the Spirit is a hard row to hoe as they say. Teach your nations about the Holy Spirit, why it's important to be baptized in the Spirit, and how to be continually filled with the Spirit (Refer back to chapter 10 for a refresher.) Some ways to help your nations cultivate a continual filling of the Spirit are to create an atmosphere of worship in your home, pray and use your prayer language together, and encourage them to take time in stillness to ask the Lord questions and then journal, draw, or talk about the visions He is relaying to them. Remaining full of the Holy Spirit will most certainly bring comfort, grace, strength, wisdom, and capability to your nations and allow their life to become an overflowing well for others to drink from.

INTO ALL THE WORLD

What a privilege it is to travel the road of raising nations; from carrying them in the womb to carrying them on our shoulders, then carrying their suitcases into college, it is an honor like no other. Many in our culture today do not understand the want or need for children, in fact more now than ever children are seen as a burden in one's life, a weight of stress, and a strain on resources. But

I truly believe that the greatest legacy man will ever leave on the earth is the treasure he's buried in the hearts of his children. We have a side-by-side participation in the greatest unfolding of God's grace that we will ever experience on this side of heaven. These nations are the torch that will be carried into all the world and into the next season of glory. As I've processed through 43 years of experiences on this earth, I have found no greater mercy of God in my life than to glimpse His heart for me through the raising of my nations. My prayer is that your heart would be enlightened to this precious truth as well.

"The greatest legacy man will ever leave in the earth is the treasure he's buried in the hearts of his children."

ABOUT THE AUTHOR

Rheanna was born and raised in Minnesota. Together with her husband, Justin, they have been raising and homeschooling their four children and just welcomed their first grand baby in December 2023! Rheanna is a best-selling author and has a bachelor's degree in theology along with an AD in Biblical Counseling from Life Christian University in Tampa, FL.

Justin and Rheanna are the co-founders and leaders of the Freedom Culture ministry, Occupy-Freedom.com, and the Occupy Freedom podcast. They have a deep passion to minister to the bound and broken and to equip God's people to acknowledge, activate, and walk in their kingdom calling, purpose & assignments.

The assignment of Freedom Culture ministries is to serve the worldwide church body as well as the local church family. Through preaching the gospel, teaching classes, counseling, mentorship strategy, podcasting, and releasing freedom through prophetic prayer ministry, Justin and Rheanna's desire is to witness the power of Christ bind the broken-hearted and set the captives free!

To contact Justin and Rheanna for more information on ministry, speaking or training opportunities, please visit the **"contact us"** tab on their website, www.occupy-freedom.com, visit Instagram **@occupyfreedompodcast**, or send an email to **myfreedomculture@gmail.com**

For more discipleship content,
check out Rheanna's best-selling book,
Polished and Concealed on Amazon.com

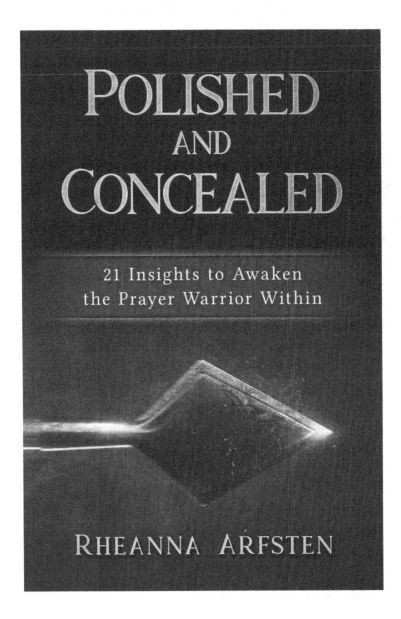

ENDNOTES

1 Dictionary.com

2 Dictionary.com

3 https://www.merriam-webster.com/dictionary/ambassador

4 Dictionary.com

5 https://en.wikipedia.org/wiki/Butterfly_effect

6 https://www.parents.com/recipes/tips/unexpected-benefits-of-eating-together-as-a-family-according-to-science/

7 https://www.forbes.com/health/mind/anxiety-statistics/#:~:text=Anxiety%20disorders%20are%20the%20most,with%206.8%20million%20adults%20affected.

8 https://www.merriam-webster.com/dictionary/friend

9 "Understanding the Teen Brain", www.urmc.rochester.edu

10 Archive youth poll: www.barna.org

11 "Meek Like a War Horse" https://www.amazon.com/Meek-Like-War-Horse-Stories/dp/1460012666/ref=sr_1_1?crid=8YU6 8OFM4LJP&dib=eyJ2IjoiMSJ9.Krk6dyKIgeQvkWuiI3X6S-SQUkuwpWrttJfa_IulD8VtcVscQtOq8o_qFbBkLHQGwUH_ TIK7tN3u_kVDA7hklgaoIpZHBLPqVwnJzIGWP8.425F7ms DIUouoL7pKM2G_qA9uv4pwgDhsHQEzX_ED-o&dib_tag= sc&keywords=sam+whatley&qid=1723164588&sprefix=sam+ whatley%2Caps%2C135&sr=8-1

12 "Bible   Archaeology   Report"   https://biblearchaeology report.com/2022/11/18/top-ten-historical-references-to-jesus-outside-of-the-bible/

13 https://koinoniafellowship.com/2018/03/24/what-does-it-mean-to-be-missional/#:~:text=As%20the%20people%20 of%20a,the%20activity%20of%20reaching%20them.

Made in the USA
Monee, IL
12 January 2025

76704194R00132